The Universe
F♥cking Loves Me

The Universe
F♥cking Loves Me

Getting Out of Your Way
and Into Your Flow

BY SARA AREY

UN-SETTLING BOOKS
Boulder, Colorado USA

Cover Designer: Sally Wright Day
Editor: Maggie McReynolds

Author's photos courtesy of
Rupa Kapoor, Woman Redefined

ISBN: 171954445X
ISBN-13: 978-1719544450

Advance Praise

You can feel Sara's smile, joy, courage, vulnerability, and acceptance of you and herself in this book. She gives us simple, practical ways to bring ourselves and our gifts to the here and now with her for-real, been-there-done-that understanding of what we're going through. Her experiences have been all the way from sad and touching to funny and "no, duh!" Sara's warm welcome for us to shine comes right from her heart...along with the powerful love from the Universe.

    —Tapas Fleming, L.Ac.
       Founder, TAT® at TATLife.com

If you've ever felt stuck in your own stuff, read this book. If you've ever felt like you're in your own way, this book is for you. For anyone who hasn't had the good fortune to work with Sara in person yet, this book is a powerful intro to that experience—and to the difference it makes in your ability to show up in your own life.

For those who feel stuck in their own stuff, including the growing number of people—like me—who've been lucky enough to experience Sara's work first-hand, this book is a wonderful resource and handbook—a reminder of the empowering concepts of Sara's Refuturing Process, coaching prompts you can put into play immediately, powerful metaphors that open your mind, stories that give you insight—AND it's a great read!

—Deborah Henson-Conant
Grammy-Nominated Composer, Performer,
Speaker, & Coach at HipHarp.com

Ms. Arey has written a guide for all of us who think we've broken the Law of Attraction. Far from living in a hostile universe, she tells us, the Universe fucking loves us, just as it loves her. We just need to understand how these messages of love arrive and manifest in our world. And in this gem of a book, she shows us how to do just that.

—Jeanne Andrus
The Menopause Guru
and author of I Just Want to Be ME Again!

If you think the title's great, just wait 'til you read the book.

—Lori Barklage
Owner, Ancient Art Midwifery Institute

This book is a must-read for anyone who feels like they've been forgotten or slighted by The Universe. Sara's stories illustrate in a simple and powerful way how the only thing that's real in this world is how much we are loved. Period.

—Christine Springer
CEO & Founder of Christine Springer Coaching,
ChristineSpringerCoaching.com

For Trey, Maylen, and Bri

And the Universe

Thank you for loving me

Contents

Foreword

By Christine Kane
PRESIDENT AND FOUNDER, UPLEVEL YOU

If there's one thing our funny little egos clamor for, it's a good label. There's nothing like the perfect box to put someone in.

- *"Ah, an accountant. Safe and uninteresting."*

- *"A hippie. Loose, irresponsible, and needs a better deodorant."*

- *"A priest. Hmmm, maybe I should walk the other way."*

Never mind accuracy. Egos want to know how to judge the situation and each player involved.

So, as someone who founded what is now a multi-million-dollar, business-coaching company—Uplevel You—I occasionally have to deflect the all-too-common, left-brain labels that go with the territory. Labels like "Strategy," "Systems," "Sales," or "Spreadsheets." At a photo shoot years ago, the photographer shouted at me to "look more like an executive!" while showing me how I should stand: arms crossed in various power poses.

At the same time, I often find myself being asked to justify the spiritual or soul practices I've incorporated into my business trainings. A word like "spiritual" evokes a whole different set of categories and rules than a word like "business." Spiritual people should wear loose-fitting clothes and sensible shoes and talk in hushed, breathy tones. They most certainly don't swear. Or talk about money. So they can't be business people. (Well, maybe they run a non-profit, but not with any semblance of order.)

When people find out that I coach my business clients on two tracks—the Strategy Track and the Soul Track—they either turn away like they've just met the crazy cat lady on the block...or they seem totally relieved and they lean in. The ones who lean in know there's truth in the idea that their own energy and mindset (the spiritual) make an impact not just their business, but their whole life.

Sara Arey had a lot to do with my being able to unshackle the Soul Track from kneejerk labels, solidify it so it could be put into practice, and give it legitimate and equal status alongside the hard business strategies I teach.

Sara was the very first coach I hired at Uplevel You. I'd always been deliberate and unapologetic about incorporating soul work into our processes—it was (and still is) a big reason clients sought us out. (Hey, all the strategies in the world can't help you or your company if you keep getting stuck in your old stories.) Though I didn't know it then, bringing Sara on board quickly became our next step in elevating that spiritual side of our work with clients.

Sara's superpower is unsticking stuck people. With great intuition, and a carefully developed and proven process, Sara gets you out of your own way and into your flow—which, for most of us, is reason enough to read this book.

Working with Sara, our clients learned to reframe expectations into invitations, rid themselves of paralyzing judgment and shame, and turn demanding goals into enticing choices. With Sara, they were able to open to something so much bigger than their restricted egos had ever imagined for them.

Within several sessions, our clients experienced transformative results in their businesses and their lives. Tangible ones such as profit growth. And intangible ones such as personal growth. In those early years, it wasn't unusual to overhear people at our events sharing the "magic" Sara had worked on them. My inbox filled up with OMG messages about her.

Their success was the eye-opener I needed to see that this soul work was more than just a slice of entrepreneurial training—it was its own full track. And clients needed to attend to it and work it just as much, if not more, than the Strategy Track. With Sara's astute input, I laid out the first teachings and tools of Uplevel You's now celebrated Soul Track.

Sara's remarkable ability to help people shift out of painful patterns is, I believe, a direct outgrowth of her world view. Many gurus teach that this life we live is some kind of Universe University, with endless lessons to be learned, challenging tests to judge our worth, and success or failure being the final measure. To them, being successful means thinking positively at all times, chanting affirmations with conviction whether or not we believe we can achieve them, and daily striving to be better, bigger, or at least MORE than we are right now, damn it.

Sara doesn't buy into that whole stressful and often defeating way of looking at the world. As she sees it—and as she shows you throughout this book—we're already exactly who we should be. Life is simply our opportunity to expand, to move even closer to our essence and experience the divine within us, if we accept the invitation to do so. And if you're reading this book, I'm betting you've already RSVP'd in the affirmative.

As Sara so often and elegantly states, "The purpose of life is to live." And in the pages of this book, she lays out positive, sure, and potent ways to do that fully. You learn her subtle and effective techniques—such as Refuturing—to rid yourself of patterns and thoughts that keep you stuck. She teaches you to move forward, not with oppressive goals, but through more centering "I Choose" statements. Mostly, you learn to take joy in life, own your power, be present, and feel to your very core that "The Universe Does Fucking Love You." And with that, the world—this life, your life—becomes truly yours to experience, to love, and to realize however you wish.

How do I know? Well, I have many hundreds of clients whose successful businesses and successful lives can attest to the revolutionary power of Sara's methods. But

I really know because I have found them instrumental in my own expansion and continue to practice them myself.

So turn the page already. I'm excited for you. Because you, my dear reader, are on the threshold of expansion.

Introduction

If you're like my clients, you've read about energy and manifestation. You try to live right, to be positive, and to do some good in the world.

And some days, it feels like too freaking much.

You might be like the woman I talked to recently who *loved* the title of this book, saying, "That's it, isn't it? The Universe *does* fucking love me." As the conversation went on, she told me about how hard things are right now, how frustrated she is, how she's read *The Secret* more than once, and it just doesn't seem to work for her. There's both the knowing that she's loved by the Universe, and the sense of not experiencing it in her life—at least, not in the ways she wants to.

I get that. My own relationship with the Universe has been a work in process for a long time.

I grew up in a small Southern town surrounded by family—Mom and Dad, sisters, grandparents, an aunt and uncle, cousins. Not only do we love each other, we really *like* each other. My sisters and cousins have always been some of my best friends.

This should have given me a deep sense of security and well-being. In some respects, it did, and I know I was really, really lucky. But there was another side too.

Ever since I can remember, I've had a deep sense being different, of being out of step with everyone around me. I never felt really *seen* or that I could fully be myself, whatever *that* was.

I went through a time when I was six or seven of going to the front of the house after everyone was asleep and crying so that I wouldn't disturb anyone. I don't remember now why I was crying, except that it felt like my heart was breaking. I have no idea why I didn't tell my parents. In fact, I didn't tell anyone at all until maybe ten years ago.

Another thing I didn't tell anyone was that I was having some strange experiences. One was when I was in my room one afternoon when I was around nine. I was sitting in front of a mirror and felt God's presence really strongly. In my head, in a way that was more knowing than hearing, I felt God say that there was a purpose to my life. I didn't know specifically what that purpose was, but I had the sense that it would unfold over time. I knew that this path wouldn't always be easy, and that it would make a difference. I clearly remember saying somewhat nervously, "OK, I'll do it, just don't make me do it alone."

What I felt then—and called God—I've since come to call by many names, including God, the Universe, the Divine, Love, and All That Is. This presence is so all-encompassing that words seem inadequate and irrelevant. Throughout this book, feel free to substitute the name(s) you like and feel comfortable with.

This feeling of being different and not fitting in continued. Most people didn't know about it. I learned to gloss over it. I was happy. I did well in school and had good friends. And in the midst of it all, there was a deep current of disconnection that led to feelings of resentment and jealousy, which I also worked hard not to show.

Somewhere along the way, I discovered a deep desire to understand life and our greater purpose here. I had a compelling yearning to connect and love in a truly meaningful way. Surface-level wasn't for me. I wanted to be connected to the Divine, to myself, and to others with all of my being.

This desire is so strong that it's made it easy to say yes to anything that might lead me closer to living this way.

When my aunt introduced me to Reiki in 1990, I jumped at the chance to take a workshop and ended up eventually getting my Master level.

When a friend told me about the transformational work of the Landmark Forum, I was at the workshop four days later.

When a friend told me that his wife taught tai chi, I got enough people interested for her to start a new round of classes that month.

When another friend got certified in hypnosis and asked if she could show me what to do so that we could hypnotize each other, I agreed, and we started that night.

Reality Strikes

While all of this was going on, there were other realities too. My husband and I had some real challenges

3

in our marriage. We had a lot to learn about being in a healthy, happy relationship, and we had some experiences that felt like "real life" crashing in. For instance, we had a daughter, Bri, who was born three months early and weighed just over two pounds. Other than forgetting to breathe so often that she was known as the apnea queen in the hospital, she did well and came home only seven weeks later.

Our second daughter, Margaret Alice, was born even earlier and weighed less than two pounds. She also had a severe lung infection. She died the next day as I held her for the first and only time.

In the first months after Margaret Alice's death, all I could see was the pain and heartache. I had done everything I knew to do to have a safe pregnancy and a healthy baby. My heart was broken, and I no longer trusted the Divine in the same way. While I loved my older daughter and husband, and felt loved and held by family and friends, it felt like I had a gaping hole in my heart.

I was angry. Angry with the doctors, with Margaret Alice, with myself, with my body, with my husband...and I was really angry with the Universe.

I thought we had a deal, the Universe and I. I thought we agreed that I would do what the Universe wanted me to do and that I wouldn't have to do it alone. While I had known that my life wouldn't be easy, it never occurred to me that this much pain would be part of my path. We were buddies, the U and I, weren't we? How in the hell could one buddy do something like this to the other? Or if not directly do it, then allow it to happen? This was not the act of a loving friend. I felt betrayed and angry. As I'd done with my feeling of being different, I buried my anger, but it was definitely still there.

Along with those feelings was the knowledge that there had to be more to this than I understood. In addition to feeling hurt and mad, I felt hopeful and willing to understand more. I was *willing* to have a new perspective.

Healing Wounds

The following analogy is a little gross, and I apologize if that bothers you. I've just never found one that's better.

It's as though these thoughts and beliefs, about ourselves and about how life should be, create a small wound, like a cut on the body. If it doesn't heal well, it becomes infected. If we cover it over with what looks like shiny, healthy skin, the infection doesn't heal. It just goes deeper.

Left untreated, this becomes an abscess, but all on the inside. You see the signs of it—a rising temperature, soreness in the area, and a rising white blood cell count—but you may not know where the infection site is, especially if it's been well-concealed. To heal the abscess, you need to cut through the covering and let all of that gunk out, exposing it to air and light.

I had covered over my sense of never fitting in and of being "different." My sense of being weak. I'd done a decent job of fitting in, and I really was happy on many levels. I had family and friends whom I loved, and I'd started exploring energy work. Life would have been OK, fine even, had I kept going that way.

5

The big thing was that I wasn't being fully myself. To live the life my soul was longing to live, I had to be more me. It's in looking back that the pieces have fully fallen into place.

What I couldn't see then, and am truly only getting as I write this book, is that Margaret Alice's death opened a connection to that old sense of separation and disconnection I'd had as a child, the one I'd smoothed over and told myself was OK. In grieving for her, I was able to finally grieve and shed the tears from my deep sense of not fitting in.

This experience, and the spiritual journey it set me on, has taught me things I couldn't have learned any other way. I see how each step was guided. I see that I was held and loved by the Universe, even and especially in the times that felt the darkest. When I needed someone to guide me, the optimal person showed up. Each experience I needed to have unfolded at the perfect time. It truly was a dance between the Universe and me. The Universe gave me gift after gift, and I said yes each time.

In the months following Margaret Alice's death, a new friend, Lori, offered to do a technique with me that she'd learned called Tapas Acupressure Technique® (TAT®). I said yes. A few years later, the originator, Tapas Fleming, came to our area to do a workshop. I signed up. During the workshop, Tapas said that she needed help with her business and asked if anyone was interested in working with her. Lori and I raised our hands.

Several years later, I was looking back through my

records for something and realized that the day I said yes to joining Tapas's team was Margaret Alice's birthday. Of course. Margaret Alice's life and death, just as they were, were a gift to me that helped me on my path in ways I couldn't have predicted.

Walking My Talk

I'm committed to authenticity, which means I'm constantly doing my own work of releasing and expansion. I did TAT for myself virtually every day for over eight years. I made lists and lists of my beliefs, thoughts, fears, and identifications and then cleared them. I even did TAT once on not wanting to do TAT about a situation. This all comes from my deep desire to create an excellent life for myself, one in which I have excellent relationships and am fully myself. I can't do that while holding onto old baggage.

What I discovered was that I was never, ever broken. Broken open, yes. Broken, no. I learned that what created that covered-over, unhealed emotional infection was my belief that there was something wrong with me. The infection wasn't caused by what had happened, but by the way I'd held onto and internalized it. When I got to the heart of the pain, all I found was light and love and me.

As part of my work for Tapas, I attended almost all of her workshops, both online and in person. I especially loved her Spiritual Retreats, where we combined TAT and a method of deep self-exploration to create direct experiences of consciousness.

At one of the Spiritual Retreats, I asked the Divine,

"What is love?" All of a sudden, all of my awareness was centered inside my mouth. A sweetness more pure and transcendent than anything I've ever experienced filled my mouth. I cried at the overwhelming deliciousness of this sweet love. It seemed to fill every cell of my tongue and my mouth until everything else disappeared. It wasn't just a taste of sweetness, either. It was a vibration that my entire being had begun resonating with. And then it hit me like a bolt of lightning—nothing had been added to my mouth. This sweetness, this love, was who I already was. This is who I am. This is what I'm made of. Love.

At another retreat, we were working in pairs. With my eyes closed, I asked, "Who is the other?" in the sense of *who are other people?* I slowly opened my eyes, then had to shut them immediately. The beauty and radiance of my partner was literally too much for me to look at. His divinity was shining so brightly it was like trying to look at the sun from two feet away. I tried opening my eyes with my head turned but had the same experience every time I saw someone.

For over an hour, all I could do was sit with my eyes closed and sob at the sheer beauty of every single being around me. I have tears now writing this and remembering what it was like to see us as God does—to literally see the radiance of God shining from everyone around me. And it wasn't just certain people. It was

every.

single.

person.

This is how I *know* that you are loved, that the Universe fucking loves you. I've seen how it sees you and how heartbreakingly beautiful you are. We are *all* this beautiful. We are all made of love.

Do I see this way all day every day? No, I definitely still have times of seeing with my human eyes. And at the same time, I can never be away from this for too long. Having these experiences made these understandings of love and who we are a part of my being.

Each of those opportunities and each of my yeses created the life and business I have today. My clients can feel how deeply I know that they are worthy and beautiful because it's not just in the words, it's in my energy.

I work to keep reconnecting with this knowing. When I build up ideas or hold onto thoughts that aren't in alignment with this knowing, I consciously work to let go of that stuff. Heck, writing this book is a part of my process of realignment.

For most of us, the biggest challenge is seeing our own beauty and worthiness, at least it has been for me. It takes real work some days, and I keep doing that work.

I now get that feeling different is part of my gifts. I see life from a different perspective than most people, and *that's OK*. More and more, I'm honoring my differences and doing what I need to do to support my energy.

For instance, I know that when I go on group retreats, I'm likely to sleep very little. The energy feels so intense to me that I have a hard time falling asleep, and then I often wake up after just a few hours. Now, I no longer fight it or resent the fact that I'm awake. Instead, I enjoy the time. I go outside, I dance, sing, meditate, and do energy work. Not only is it fun, it helps me process all that energy. And I nap when I can.

I cry when I see beauty, especially the beauty of human connection and acts of generosity and courage, and I no longer work so hard to hide my tears. I adore deeply connecting with people and talking about something that one or both of us are passionate about. When I feel dragged down by someone else's fear or resistance to change, I do what I need to in order to take care of myself.

The biggest thing I've gotten at a deep, cellular level over the last few years is that even in my darkest moments, I am held and loved. The more I relax into that, the more I experience ease and flow in my life. Even when things feel hard or look scary, when I relax, breathe, and take one step at a time, things work out. Always.

Loving and embracing who I am is huge, and it's powerful. It's what allows me to show up in my life in bigger and bigger ways.

Increasing my awareness and owning my power has been my life's work. It's what I'm most passionate about helping others do too. This book is a way for me to share what I've learned so that you, too, can feel more and more in the flow of life. You have gifts and a purpose to your life. Your soul wants to express itself and live a full life with more fun, ease, and grace. What I've learned can help you do just that.

My intention and hope are that in reading this book, you get a deeper and deeper sense that the Universe fucking loves you. I hope that every time you see or hear this phrase, it resonates in whatever way you need it to in that moment, whether you're celebrating it, acknowledging a simple truth, or holding onto it like a lifeline. It's true.

The Universe fucking loves you.

The Universe fucking loves me.

The Universe fucking loves us.

Lightning Bolts
of DUH

Because you picked up this book, some part of you must resonate with the thought that the Universe fucking loves you. You may have felt an inner voice saying, "Yes, it does!" You probably smiled because it feels good to acknowledge it. You may well have had a sense of warmth and peace.

As you sat with it, though, you likely also felt uneasy. The unease may have felt small and distant, or it may have been big and in your face. A lot depends on what you've had going on lately.

It can be confusing to have so many mixed feelings. Life feels good, with positive things happening, and at the same time it feels hard, maybe even really hard.

- You may love your business and also be worried about where the money's going to come from.

- You may love someone and be super frustrated at how they're pushing your buttons.

- You may like your life and also feel a vague sense of being lost.

You may have lost your job and be happy because you really didn't like it—and also scared because you don't know what to do now.

You may know that the Universe loves you, but damn, some days it just doesn't *feel* like it when you get hit by something hard. This is how most of my clients are feeling when we start working together. One of my favorite things in the world is the moment when they have a big aha and things shift. Their faces become radiant. They're often crying, laughing, or both, and they have a new clarity and ease about them.

When you have that "aha" moment, you feel so excited! This is HUGE! A game-changer. Then you're struck by the thought, "This sounds so stupid. Of *course* this is true. I already knew this."

It feels both life-changing and anticlimactic.

Here's why this happens: *We know truths on different levels.* We typically think of knowing as black and white. You know something, or you don't. That was definitely true in school, right? In reality, though, there are many levels of knowing.

You can divide the levels of knowing into three major categories: **MIND, HEART,** and **BODY.**

Mind Knowing

Mind knowing is when you understand something intellectually. These are things you've learned because someone told you they were true. This is the depth at which you know much of what you learned in school. For instance, you know the Earth is round at a mind level.

At some point, someone told you that the Earth is round. You trusted them enough, or they had enough evidence, that you believed them. You've seen globes. You may even have flown to the other side of the world without finding any edges, but you don't have *direct* experience of its roundness. You haven't held it, rolled it, or spun it.

Heart Knowing

When you know something at the level of your heart, you know it emotionally. You know you love someone because you *feel* it, not because someone explained it to you.

Blaise Pascal famously said, "The heart has its reasons of which the reason knows nothing." I'd say that "the heart has its truths of which the mind is unaware."

Body Knowing

The deepest knowing is body knowing. This is different from knowing something intuitively at gut level or having a gut instinct about something. When I talk about body knowing, I mean that you know it in your *whole* body at a cellular, visceral level. This is knowing something at an energetic level. It's in your being and in your vibration.

Knowing something fully at this level means that there's no room for doubt. You consistently act on the knowing without hesitation. This level of knowing comes from a direct experience of the truth.

Let's go back to the example of your intellectual

understanding of the Earth being round. Astronauts have a different level of knowing about the roundness of the Earth. They don't *believe* the Earth is round, they *know* from experience that it is. They've seen it. For them, the roundness of the Earth is no longer academic. It's become a visceral knowing.

I can imagine the first astronauts looking out the window of the rocket and saying, "OMG! The Earth is round!!"

This is what a spiritual aha is—when something you mentally *believe* becomes something you viscerally *know*.

I call these experiences **Lightning Bolts of Duh.** Or being gobsmacked by the obvious.

Here's an example: Vanessa was incredibly frustrated when we started our call. She was feeling guilt, shame, and fear over having taken a job for which she had been "*ridiculously* underpaid" and then quitting it. As she released her self-hatred and inner struggle, she remembered that she had taken the job after leaving an abusive relationship. She felt her heart opening as her compassion for herself grew. She was able to appreciate her courage in doing something to take care of herself at a time when she felt so defeated, even if the job was less than ideal.

We kept working and her awareness moved from being all in her head to being down in her body. That's the feeling of becoming more centered and grounded. She got, at a deep level, that she hadn't "lost ground" by working at that job or by leaving it. She was simply taking one step and then another. Taking the job was a step in caring for herself. Leaving it was a step in her valuing herself and her time.

She now knows in her heart and body that this is all working out for her highest good.

If I had told her this at the beginning of our call, she would have nodded in agreement. Of course that's true. Yet she was still worrying and struggling because that knowing was only brain-deep.

She now has this knowing in all of her.

Remember when I shared about experiencing that my very cells vibrate at the level of love and actually seeing that every being is stunningly, breathtakingly beautiful in their Divine radiance? Those experiences were significant because they took mental beliefs to the level of cellular knowing. Those experiences changed my vibration and are now reflected in my energy. Clients can feel this in me, even though they have no idea exactly what they're sensing or why.

Here's another example to help with this distinction.

Is ice cold?

Do you *believe* that ice is cold, or do you *know* it is?

When you're hot and want to cool down, do you reach for a glass of water with or without ice? Do you have to stop and think about it? Would you take a free webinar that promises to teach you that ice is cold? Of course not—because you know in every part of you that ice is cold. You've experienced it over and over and over.

This knowing is so deep that if anyone tried to convince you that ice is hot, you'd just laugh. You wouldn't even be upset because that's so clearly not true. There's absolutely no room for doubt about the coldness of ice. This is what I call Level 5 body knowing.

Here's the scale I use with clients

I know this in my mind.	I know this in my heart.	I know this in my body.
0 1 2 3 4 5	0 1 2 3 4 5	0 1 2 3 4 5

0-nope   1-rarely   2-sometimes   3-frequently   4- almost always   5-YES!

Let's take the statement, "I am worthy of abundance." Do you know that? If so, how deeply do you know it?

When you know something at a Level 1 to Level 4, you're sometimes in your knowing, and sometimes not. You might feel confident that you're worthy of abundance when you get a nice check, and then deeply doubt it when you think of asking for a raise.

Knowing something at a Level 5 in all three areas means that you act on it every time without hesitation, like how you reach for ice when you want to cool down with a deep, unshakable confidence that it'll help. This is visceral knowing.

When your mind, heart, and body knowing are aligned, you are unstoppable in that knowing.

Think about Vanessa's realization. How deeply do you know that what you're experiencing now is part of a bigger process that is working out for your highest good? (Hint: If you're struggling with the situation, it's not a Level 5 in all three areas.)

I love the title of this book, in part because it's so much about these levels of knowing.

Often, I say it in celebration, like when a new client signs on or when I get the last seat on a nonstop cross-country flight. Sometimes there are even a few dance moves involved. At those moments, I know it in my heart.

I've even been known to say it through gritted teeth, a reminder that, as my mother says, this too shall pass, and everything will work out, no matter how it looks in this moment. At these moments, I'm working to get it more deeply in my mind and more deeply in my heart.

There've also been times when I've said it late at night, when the worries have felt so big and I've felt so small. At those times, I said like a mantra, reminding myself and bringing me comfort.

Those times when I've whispered it into the dark have taught me the most about the Universe's love. It's then that I surrender and accept what's going on. I then feel a peace that's beyond anything I could create myself. As I take my next steps trustingly and watch as the pieces fall into place, my knowing about the Universe's love moves even deeper.

Imagine knowing 100 percent,
in an ice-is-cold, Level-5-in-all-areas way,
that the Universe fucking loves you.
You know it so deeply that it never even
enters your mind not to act on it.

Knowing it that way means you'd never hesitate to show up. You'd know that you couldn't fail because the Universe fucking loves you. You'd never believe something "wasn't working out" because you'd know that everything always does, even if you don't understand it yet with your human perspective. You'd never be afraid of anyone's rejection or judgment, and there'd be nothing to worry about or fear. Ever. You'd have a permanent safety net beneath you at all times.

The way to get to this type of knowing is by *experiencing* something over and over and over. Each experience takes it deeper and deeper until it's a part of your energy and who you are. You exude it, acting on it without thinking or wavering.

The question isn't, "Do you know that the Universe fucking loves you?", but rather, "How *deeply* do you know it?" And what's in the way of your knowing it more thoroughly?

The great thing about the Universe is that the Universe doesn't give up on us. It's not petty and vengeful the way one of us might be. It never doesn't love us, whether we're open to receiving it or not.

It patiently waits for us to create an opening to receive its love, the love that it's always, always expressing. That's all.

The more we trust, the more open and receptive we are. The more open and receptive we are, the more the Universe can give to us.

Sound Familiar?

For a long time, I said I trusted the Universe while making a plan B. Essentially, I was saying, "I trust you, you're great, and if you don't come through for me, I've got it." That's like doing a trust fall while still holding onto a safety bar. It just doesn't work. And it leaves your partner standing there with their arms outstretched, waiting.

There were times when the fall didn't seem so big, or when the decision seemed so clear that it was easy to trust. After Margaret Alice's death, I was told by my doctor not to get pregnant again. We knew our family wasn't complete, so we began looking into adoption. We were planning to adopt domestically until I saw our daughter three times during meditation, and she was Chinese. I didn't feel any doubt about taking this step. I'd seen our daughter. She was very real to me.

A year later in a hotel room halfway around the world, when we held Maylen for the first time, we discovered that she has a birthmark that's identical to the one our oldest daughter Bri has. It felt like the Universe was saying, "See? You were meant for each other. I've got this."

At other times, I could only trust the Universe so far. Those were the times when I worried a lot. I made plans and took actions, not because they felt resonant or exciting for me, but because it seemed like a "smart" move. I was trying to maintain control.

Then came a cascade of events that wrenched my hand off the safety bar. One of my girls went through a really tough and sometimes scary period. At the same time, we had financial challenges like we'd never had before. I couldn't come up with a fix for all of that. My choices were to surrender to life or fight for control.

When you read "surrender," you might have thought I meant "giving up." That's not what I mean. I wasn't giving up in the sense of sitting down by the side of the road and waiting to be rescued. Not at all.

What I mean by surrender is surrendering control. I surrendered my thinking that I had to, or even could, "fix" all of that. I even surrendered my thinking that there was anything wrong. Instead, I embraced what was happening, trusting that there was a gift in the situation, just as it was.

I prayed over and over, "Universe, break me open. Help me know who I really am. Help me trust you. Help me experience your love for me in bigger, deeper ways."

Wow, did the Universe deliver. So many old, old fears dissolved as I experienced magic in the midst of mayhem.

Sometimes the dissolving came through tears and being broken open in ways that felt like my heart broke. Sometimes it came through laughter, connection, and experiences of being deeply seen and held. Sometimes it came from my continuing to take one step at a time toward what called to my heart and felt expansive, even when those steps felt intense and challenging.

And I wouldn't trade a minute of it.

In June of 2017, I wrote this on Facebook:

Yesterday was the 19th anniversary of my second daughter's birth. Today is the anniversary of her death.

I went for a long time feeling "done" with my grieving. Then I went through a spell of really deep grieving a year or two ago. For months, deeper and deeper levels emerged. Of course, I was grieving a lot of things around Margaret Alice's death, and so much more as well. Sometimes grieving for her was a doorway to grieve other things, and to connecting with the purest, rawest emotions that sometimes had no name.

Today, instead of grief, I feel profound gratitude. Gratitude for the whole experience of her life. Gratitude for the course my healing set me on, and the work I do now as a result of it. Gratitude for the love and support that's surrounded me through all of this. Gratitude for the amazing daughters I get to see and hug, and for how opening my heart to my grief has opened it to deeper love as well.

I'm grateful for this experience because when I look into the eyes of someone who's in deep pain, I can go there with them. I know this terrain, and I don't shy away from it. I know its pain and I know its gifts. And I know in my bones that even the worst of experiences can bring us more into our own power, if we understand how to navigate them.

Margaret Alice taught me how to say goodbye and let go. To trust that even in partings there is growth and beauty. To open my heart when my head wants to shut it down and to not feel the intensity.

I would not have consciously chosen this experience—then or now. It was devastatingly hard at times. And I embrace it, because it's

the truth. And because in embracing it, I stop
struggling inside.

This is what I mean by surrender. This is what I mean by knowing deeply that we are loved and held, even in the darkest of times. This is what can lead us to our greatest joy and deepest fulfillment—not by fighting life and challenges, but by embracing them.

What Am I
Doing Wrong?

If you're like a lot of people I know, you've heard about manifesting and been trying some of its principles.

You've worked hard to be really specific about what you want. You've visualized it. You've kept your thoughts positive. You've told yourself that it's on the way to you. You've worked really hard at it.

And it's not working like you'd hoped. The money, the new relationship, the new car hasn't shown up. You feel discouraged and a little bit pissed (or maybe a lot pissed). The experts say it's easy to manifest. Apparently, it is—for them.

Or maybe you can do it in some areas or have been able to do it in the past, but there's something for which it ain't happening. Argh! It's so frustrating! And this leaves you with the question, "What am I doing wrong?"

You may not like this answer, but here it is: That's not an effective question. It makes sense that you're asking it. We're used to trying to solve problems. That's why we have brains, right? We need to fix what's wrong, and then life gets better. If something isn't working in our lives, we fix it. Tweak it. Improve it.

Makes sense, right?

Except for this: Focusing on what's wrong keeps you right where you are. It keeps your energy at the level of the problem, not the solution. That's the opposite of what you need for creating what you want.

The more you focus on what's wrong, the more stuck you stay.

The other problem with focusing on what's wrong is that you miss what the Universe is trying to give you. It's like the Universe brings you flowers, and you're upset that they're not chocolates. Or a car. So you push away the flowers and say, "I want a car!"

Now imagine what a human lover would do if this pattern of ignoring or disregarding gifts kept repeating. That lover would give up, right? Fortunately, the Universe is infinitely patient and continues to give to you. That's the best news there is.

Try this. Focus on something that's going wrong in your life. Now, let your attention wander over your body and just see what you notice.

There was tension, right? And probably general heaviness. Those are signs that you're carrying energetic "weight." They show that your energy is vibrating at a low frequency.

Imagine that there's a pipe connecting you to the Universe. The Universe delivers what you need through this pipe.

The heaviness you felt is like gunk clinging to the sides of the pipe. In some places, there may only be a little gunk. In other places, it's really thick. And what does that gunk do? It narrows the pipe, so less can get through to you.

That gunk is the S.T.U.F.F. you carry around.

S.T.U.F.F. stands for **Stuck Thoughts, Unresolved Feelings, and Fears.**

S.T.U.F.F.

Stuck
Thoughts,
Unresolved
Feelings, and
Fears

In your head, your S.T.U.F.F. will show up as thoughts like:

- This probably isn't going to work for me. It sure hasn't been working.

- What if I'm asking for the wrong thing?

- This feels too easy. Anything that's worth having is worth working hard for.

- Everyone else seems to have it easier than me. They probably know something I don't.

In your body, it shows up as the tension and heaviness we were talking about before.

In your emotions, it shows up as fear, anger, depression, and sadness.

The more S.T.U.F.F. you clear away, the more open the pipe is and the more that can come to you.

Asking, "What am I doing wrong?" has you focusing on the gunk, which lowers your vibration and holds the gunk in place. It's like it makes the sides of the pipe stickier so the gunk attaches more firmly.

Focusing on what's working does the opposite. It raises your vibration, making it harder for the gunk to hang on. It's like having two magnets pulling toward each other, and slowly turning one so that it starts to repel the other. Your positive outlook makes it harder for the fears and worries to hang on.

Funnily enough, this can feel very uncomfortable or even scary. It's different. You've had these worries and fears for a long time as a type of protection. You might worry that without them, you won't know who you are, you'll make the same mistakes again or you'll be without protection that you need. As worry and fear start to go, you may grab them back without even realizing you're doing it.

Often, releasing S.T.U.F.F. includes tears. If there was strong emotion in the gunk like anger, hurt, or fear, the release may be equally strong. Feeling these strong emotions can be very uncomfortable, so often the knee-jerk reaction is to shut it down. We do this by holding our breaths, tensing our muscles, or distracting ourselves. And guess what that does? It keeps the gunk in place!

The most powerful, freeing thing you can do is to let yourself get uncomfortable and *feel*.

Does that make you want to throw up, or throw this book across the room? I get it. I'm not going to lie to you. Feeling your feelings can be intense and painful. There's a reason you stuck that S.T.U.F.F. to the funnel instead of letting it flow through in the first place!

Not feeling it, though, keeps your pipe clogged. The way to release it is to feel it. Feel and let flow.

The heavier it is and the more intense the release, the greater your sense of freedom and lightness will be on the other side. You'll feel the spaciousness that's opened up. Your body will relax, and you'll breathe more deeply. The releasing will be more intense too.

Keep in mind that you can start with the smaller stuff and go slowly, especially if you've had some really heavy experiences in your life. This isn't a race. It's a process. And you can get help. Help and support can make all the difference in the world.

To start, focus on the evidence that the Universe fucking loves you. A gratitude journal where you write down five things a day that you're grateful for is a great way to do this. Studies have shown that, when people keep gratitude journals, they become happier. Even their friends and family report a difference in them. This is because focusing on gratitude raises your vibration, and a higher vibration means less gunk in your pipe, so more gifts from the Universe can get through.

When you start from the belief that the Universe fucking loves you, everything gets turned around. You don't have to *work* to manifest what you want. You open to something deeper than a shopping list of "material things." You move into alignment with Life and with who you naturally are. You accept and begin moving with what's happening in your life rather than against it.

Here's another thing about letting yourself feel your emotions. The way most people approach manifestation is through their heads. They pick what they want to manifest based on what they *think* will make them happy— more money, more things, more love. These are the things that make them feel safe and secure.

Then they *think* their way to it. They make a vision board and say affirmation statements. They visualize. They focus. They work at it.

What they don't realize is that it's like they're driving a car with no gas in it. They're running on fumes and pushing it uphill. They don't know that their emotions *are* the fuel they need.

Increasing Your Energy

Your heart speaks to you through your emotions. Your soul speaks through energy. What your heart and soul want for you isn't based on material things. They want you to be fulfilled and to live a big, extraordinary life, whatever that looks like for *you*! They aren't interested in your fitting into the humdrum.

Your heart and soul aren't excited about making a poor relationship bearable. They want a relationship that expands you and brings you joy.

Your heart and soul aren't energized by a big bank statement. They're energized by you making a big difference. They get a charge each time you're authentic and do something you love. Do you feel the difference?

Discovering what your soul wants and using *that* as a focus for your vision board, then feeling your excitement as you look at it, gives energy for creation.

Doing what you have the energy and passion to do expands the pipe. And here's the real key: A wider pipe not only lets in more from the Universe, it also lets more of *you* out. You show up more in your life and in the world, and you receive more as well. Material abundance is a byproduct of living a passionate life.

As you practice this, you'll be amazed to discover how "unreal" you've been in a lot of areas of your life. You'll start to see the relationships you've hung onto that you don't really enjoy and that sap your energy. You'll start noticing what work you're doing that depletes you, and where you're being fake.

You're being fake every time you do something *in order to* make something happen. Every time you agree with someone to make them go away or be quiet. Every time you do or say something to make someone feel better. Every time you do something because you should, or you're expected to, but your heart isn't in it.

And every one of those actions costs you energy.

When you do something that's in alignment with your heart, you get energy from it. Every time you do something that's against your heart and your truth, it costs you energy. No wonder you're exhausted, right?

31

Every projection you create, like acting happy when you're miserable or acting interested when you couldn't care less, takes your energy. And if you're an entrepreneur and you're doing what an "expert" has told you to do for your business, even though it's not in alignment with your heart and who you are, that's costing you energy and clients.

Think of someone you know who you would describe as fake. How attracted to that person are you? How much do you want to be with them or work with them? How much do you trust them? Not much at all, right?

Now think of someone you know who is genuine. Keep in mind that being blunt isn't always being genuine. A lot of times, people's bluntness comes from their S.T.U.F.F., not their heart or soul. I mean someone who feels deeply authentic, grounded, and themselves.

Isn't that someone you want to be with? Someone you trust? Wouldn't you be far more likely to hire this person, to give them a gift, to invite them for coffee?

The more authentically you show up, the more you become that second person.

The more you create from your spaciousness, rather than reacting from your S.T.U.F.F., the wider your pipe and the more abundant your life.

My clients often joke that one of my superpowers is making people cry. More than once, they started when I picked up the phone and said hello. That's because my clients know that they're safe with me. They know this work takes place on an emotional and cellular level, so they can be real with me. They're letting go of the tears that are already there.

My clients also laugh in a full-bodied way with me. Being willing to let go with spontaneous, whole-hearted, nothing-held-back laughter is a much more vulnerable act than most people realize. This isn't derisive laughter, or chuckling, or a forced laugh. This is the laughter that bursts up from your heart and consumes you, and, like crying, is a way of releasing.

Look for places in your life where you feel *that* safe and can be *that* real. Honor your genuine tears and laughter.

Remember that manifestation is much more about you showing up than anything else. This means showing up in an authentic, vulnerable, powerful way. And this comes from following your heart.

As you show up more, all the issues that made it feel good to play small will come up. This is your S.T.U.F.F. That's fine. It's part of the process. Allow it to happen.

For manifestation and success in any area of your life:

1. Connect with your heart and your inner knowing to find what you're aligned with.

2. Show up authentically and take aligned action, releasing S.T.U.F.F. as it comes up.

3. Trust and be open to receive.

Why Affirmations
Backfire

You've probably heard you should use affirmations—positive statements that reinforce what you want or are trying to create. Statements like, "I am rich and abundant;" "Money flows to me with ease;" "I have all I need."

For some people, this works great. For some people, it makes things worse.

A research team at the University of Waterloo in Canada found that affirmations actually leave some people feeling *less* hopeful and *less* powerful—the opposite of what they were trying to accomplish. The really sad thing is that this happened to the people who needed help and support the most—the ones who felt the worst to start with.

Imagine being in a room that's 90°F. You're in there for several minutes, feeling the heat, sweating. Now you open the door and step into a room that's 30°F. How does your body respond to that change in temperature? By clenching, right? Even if you love the cold, your muscles tighten at the shock of the change in temperature.

Your body does this because the change is too dramatic. It's not healthy and could even cause shock or cardiac arrest, so your body does what it can to keep you safe, including fighting the change.

Your body needs you to go from 90° to 70°. Once it's used to that, you can move to 50°. When it's adjusted to 50°, you can go to 30°.

These gradual shifts keep your body from going into protective, defensive mode.

It's the same with your thoughts. When you use a statement like, "I am rich and abundant" as an affirmation when you're feeling desperate for money, it's too big a difference from your current reality. At least a part of you actively *resists* the thought.

Your mind will fight against any thought that seems "too big" or too different. It'll find evidence to disprove the too-big thought because the thought feels dangerous. A lot of people call this self-sabotage. Really, though, it's just your mind trying to protect you, trying to keep you safe.

So if affirmations don't work when you most want them to, what does? I recommend using what I call Refuturing Statements.

Refuturing Statements start out with the phrase, "What if it's possible." This phrase is open, playful, and full of, well, possibility. Even though you might mistake the Refuturing Statements for questions at first, they're stronger than that. They are proclamations of possibility, not hesitant suggestions. Therefore, they end in a period instead of a question mark.

Saying, "What if it's possible I am rich and abundant" doesn't put your mind into defensive mode. It's like changing the temperature in increments, giving your system time to adjust and even enjoy the change. You relax and open even more.

So those times I told you about before, when I was saying, "The Universe fucking loves me" into the dark, what I was actually saying was, *"What if it's possible* the Universe fucking loves me." Saying it as a certainty was just too big a leap in those moments.

Say the two statements, "I am rich and abundant" and "What if it's possible I am rich and abundant." Do you feel the difference in their energy? Which one feels lighter, more expansive? Which one leaves *you* feeling lighter and more expansive?

Using Refuturing Statements

Saying Refuturing Statements is like dropping a pebble into a still pond and watching the ripples. The energy of them creates waves on a vibrational level. As these waves move outward, they shake loose what isn't resonant with them—that old S.T.U.F.F. that had you resisting in the first place. This means that you may notice thoughts coming up that sound like objections, often starting out with words like, "What about …" or "Yeah, but …" You don't need to do anything about those. Just notice them, and then go back to the Refuturing Statement.

Even when you know something, at least somewhat, on a mental level, saying it as a definitive statement can bring up resistance on the emotional and energetic levels. You may "know" that you're awesome, yet when you look yourself in the eye in the mirror and say, "I am awesome," you notice a tightness in your chest, shallow breathing, and an impulse to look away.

Remember, if you're not acting consistently and without hesitation on something you "know," there's some part of you that *doesn't* know it. If you know something at a mind Level 3, the space between Level 3 and Level 5 is part of you doubting and second-guessing. That's the part that rejects the definitive statements.

Don't think that Refuturing Statements aren't powerful because they're gentle. The very gentleness of these statements gets them past your defenses so that they can begin shifting your S.T.U.F.F. at its roots.

On each call with my private clients, I make a recording of the Refuturing Statements I use with them. I've had clients come back to me years later to say that they still listen to their recordings, because they continue to get benefit from them. That's the statements going into deeper and deeper levels of knowing, dislodging more and more gunk from the pipe, and opening the person more and more to abundance and self-expression.

I had a client who had had a lifelong struggle with feeling safe. For months as we worked together, she would hear me say, "What if it's possible that I am safe and OK, just as I am," and she couldn't feel it. Thoughts would come up like, "But I'm not. How do you know? I've never felt safe." As I recommended, she kept listening and letting the statements wash over her. When those thoughts came up, she simply noticed them without trying to *do* anything about them, just letting them be.

Then one day we had a true breakthrough call. For the first time, she was able to share with me that her father had been mentally ill. She never knew what was going to send him into a rage. Sometimes he'd wake her up yelling at her, so she never slept well—and still didn't, even all these years later.

Like going from 90° to 30°, it was too big a shock for her system to simply say that she was safe. Her protective solution was to never fully relax, never fully trust that she was safe. Not relaxing was like wearing a coat in the 90° room, so that when she was thrust into 30°, she had the coat with her. It was a wise protective action when she was spending a lot of time in the 30° room. Now that she lives in the 90° room, it was getting in her way.

When you've had a distressful experience, some part of you feels like it's still going on long after the actual event is over. For instance, if you've been in a car wreck, your body may stiffen every time you hear brakes, waiting for impact, for months after the accident. This is self-protection. It's the survival part of us holding the belief that if it keeps reliving that experience, it stays ready in case something similar happens again.

The important message to convey to that part of us is that we're no longer in the threatening situation. It's OK to stand down. Fighting against that part, arguing that the event is over and it's crazy to keep acting this way, doesn't help.

If you've ever dealt with an angry animal, you know

that a calm demeanor and slow movements are most effective in diffusing the situation. That's like saying, "What if it's possible."

When I use Refuturing Statements with clients, I tailor them to the client's specific situation. Actually, it's more that I get them as an intuitive download. I don't plan them out or have a script I follow. Sometimes I don't even know what I'm going to say before it comes out of my mouth.

And still, there are some guidelines that can help you create your own Refuturing Statements.

- ♥ At a core level, survival is our topmost priority, so the statements generally start with, "What if it's possible that I am safe and OK." It helps settle the nervous system and create an opening for the statements that follow.

- ♥ Often, what comes next is an affirmation of the work that's been done. This addresses any self-recrimination, increases self-compassion, and decreases resistance to change. For example, "What if it's possible that I made the best decision I knew to make, and that I was doing the best I knew to do at the time."

- ♥ The statements build in certainty and depth. If someone has been really struggling with finances, saying, "What if it's possible I am rich and abundant," may be the fourth or tenth statement rather than the first one.

Refuturing Statements are also extremely potent for groups. In my Wealth School program, group calls where we clear out S.T.U.F.F. for everyone always end with Refu-turing Statements. [I call the combination of ongoing release of S.T.U.F.F. followed by affirming Refuturing Statements the Refuturing Process.]

It's amazing how much S.T.U.F.F. we have in common, including the belief that no one is as messed up as we are! While private work lets you get to the heart of what's going on for you personally, working in a group gives you access to the energy of everyone combined, which is very powerful.

From now on, I'll end each chapter with a few Refu-turing Statements. I recommend reading these statements aloud. Sound is a vibration and affects your energy in a way that simply reading them silently won't.

As a special gift, I've recorded a series of Refuturing Statements that you can download and listen to. You'll get the benefit of being able to relax and simply listen to the statements. More than that, though, you'll get my energy, which is carried in the recording. You can download the file at **theuniversefuckinglovesme.com/gift,** and play it from your phone or computer. It's yours to keep.

One word of warning: while some clients have told me that they often listen to my recordings in the car, oth-ers have told me that they become too relaxed and medi-tative to drive safely while listening. Listen the first time when you're not driving to see what works for you.

When you read or listen to the statements, you're not trying to believe them. It's more like you're just letting them wash over you. If some old, negative thoughts, feel-ings, and fears wash up in the process, just let them come up. You don't need to do anything with them or about them. Just notice them and then put your attention on the statements again.

Often, during a session, clients tell me at the end of the Refuturing Statements that they can't remember a single thing I said, yet they feel happier, lighter, more grounded, and more energized. That's fine! Sometimes clients yawn or even get teary listening to the Refuturing Statements. These are signs that big energy is shifting.

After the Refuturing Statements, we craft an "I choose" statement. This is something that they can use as a touchpoint in the coming days. It often incorporates their "lightning bolt of duh" from the session.

I've had clients keep lists of their choose statements from different calls and put them up in their office. Several clients have made memes of their statements and shared them on social media. Some put them in their journals to reread over the following days. Some have included them in artwork. One client wrote the following to me over a year after our last call:

> *I'm reviewing my two favorite "choose statements" today and feeling great depths of gratitude for your gifts. Because of you, I've opened up to so many possibilities.*
>
> *These statements that we created really keep me centered on both fronts (life and business). When I'm stressed, I read these, and they realign me. Thank you for summoning these from within me. They are still serving me well....*

"I choose to make time for quiet and for play, and I choose to allow things to be as they are."

"I choose to be compassionate with the client and situation in front of me, to support the bigger win for all of us, and to have fun doing it!"

I laugh now at the thought of "choosing" to allow things to be as they are—I mean, they're going to be that way anyway. But just saying this phrase reminds me of that reality and frees me from the struggle when I can't let things go. ☺

This person later told me that "supporting the bigger win for all of us" became the basis for his contracts with clients, showing just how helpful and practical these statements can be.

Refuturing Statements

- ♥ What if it's possible that I'm safe and OK, just as I am.

- ♥ What if it's possible that it's safe for me to relax.

- ♥ What if it's possible for me to go slowly and deeply, and that that's OK.

- ♥ What if it's possible that when I relax and have fun, I'm more creative, more magnetic, and more open to new possibilities.

43

Choose Statement

I choose to relax,
have fun,
and play with
new possibilities.

The Safety Self

My saboteur made me do it! If it weren't for my saboteurs, I'd be great. My saboteur constantly holds me back.

Ever had thoughts like these? You're not alone.

Often, when people talk about their saboteur, what they're really talking about is what I call the Safety Self. You might have heard it called the Lizard Brain. Some people refer to it as the ego.

It comes from a very old part of the brain that's often called the reptilian brain. Names like "reptilian" and "lizard" brain often have connotations of "less evolved" and "out of date." These names can lead us to dismiss that inner voice.

In fact, the most common thing I see with clients is animosity toward that inner voice. And that's understandable! It's often saying things that we don't want to hear. It talks about what could go wrong, and often encourages us to do the opposite of what we're trying to do. It speaks the language of fear and is happiest when we stay in our comfort zone and play small.

Consider this. This part of your brain has a very important function—keeping you alive. This is where your autonomic nervous system is based, the part that keeps you breathing, regulates your body temperature, and performs other vital tasks.

This part of your brain is devoted to you and your survival, which is why I call it the Safety Self. Working 24/7 to keep someone alive and healthy is a hugely loving job, as any parent can attest.

When I tell clients that this part loves them, they often do anything from chuckling disbelievingly to rolling their eyes. I get it. After all, this part is the one voicing all those negative thoughts in your head, like, "What if no one signs up to work with me? What if I can't pay my bills? What if I do all this work, and it falls flat?"

That doesn't *sound* loving at all.

Think of it this way. When this part developed, physical dangers were the main threat to life. Sure, the crystal-clear water and lush foliage outside the cave were beautiful. What was really important to notice, though, was the tiger under the bush. The job of this part of the brain was to spot the tiger.

This means that the Safety Self is *designed to look for trouble*. It's what it was built for, and it does a very fine job of pointing out potential dangers.

The problem is that we no longer live in a world where the biggest threats to our well-being are physical. Now we're much more worried about things like having enough money, taking care of loved ones, and being fulfilled.

So the Safety Self does its best to point out potential threats in today's world. And what it knows is: "Don't stand out," "Hide when scared," and "Don't take chances." That's the crux of what it says to you, isn't it?

This is its way of loving you and trying to keep you safe. Yes, it may be a sucky way of showing it, but what can it say? It's living its programming.

Most people respond in one of two ways:

1. Believe it and stay small
2. Fight it or push it away, and stay in struggle

Clearly, believing it and staying small won't get you what you want in life. You aren't here to live a small life, or you wouldn't have picked up this book.

Both pushing it away and arguing with it will only keep you engaged with it. It's not going to give up. It believes it's fighting for your life. If you've ever argued with a young child who doesn't think you're hearing her, you know what happens. She only gets *louder*! As you've probably noticed, your Safety Self responds the same way.

Plus, arguing and pushing away any part of you creates inner struggle. You're not fully aligned with your intention and your goals. Your energy is divided, and that will show up in the results (or lack of results) you get.

So what other option is there?

Listen to it.

"What?" you say. "But you said that wouldn't work. Option #1, remember?"

Listening and buying into (believing) are two different things. This is a lesson my child taught me.

When my kids were young, we were driving home one afternoon when one of them decided that she wanted to have ice cream for supper. On that night, it wasn't going to happen. At first, I tried reasoning with her, telling her why we need wholesome food. You can imagine how well that went over. Next, I tried ignoring her. She just got louder and more insistent. Finally, I said, "You really want ice cream for supper."

"Yes", she said in a teary voice.

"It would be fun and taste good."

"Yes."

"We're having soup tonight and I'm really looking forward to it. I wonder, if we *were* having ice cream, what flavor would you want?"

We then went on to have a conversation about ice cream flavors, what everyone's favorites were, how many scoops we'd have, etc. We had a fun drive home because my daughter felt heard, and we ate soup for dinner.

Now, I'm not saying you need to have an in-depth conversation with your Safety Self. In fact, all you need to do is to listen. You can do what I have all my clients do: Invite those thoughts up by simply asking, "And what else?" until your Safety Self has said all it wants to say.

One hundred percent of the time, clients report feeling more calm and relaxed. The Safety Self quiets down because it did its job of delivering the warning. Very often, those inner conversations end with my client feeling a connection with a scared, child-part. This is like turning on the light and looking under the bed to confront the monster only to find that it's your cat.

When you know that the Universe fucking loves you, that means *all* of the Universe, including that voice inside you. When you can hear the love, you can acknowledge and *let go of* the things it says that don't seem like real dangers to you. If it warns you not to walk in front of a stampeding herd of rhinos, by all means listen to that one.

Another way to respond is with Refuturing Statements. If your Safety Self says, "What if this doesn't work?" try saying, "I hear that you're scared. What if it's possible that it *will* work. What if it's possible that I can do this." Remember, you're not arguing. You're hearing and acknowledging the fears, and then inviting your Safety Self to be in the realm of possibilities with you.

Refuturing Statements

♥   What if it's possible that it's OK for me
    to feel nervous or even scared.

♥   What if it's possible that feeling nervous
    and scared doesn't mean something's wrong.

♥   What if it's possible that feeling nervous
    and scared means I'm doing something new,
    and that that's OK.

♥   What if it's possible that it's OK for me
    to breathe and relax.

♥   What if it's possible this can work.

♥   What if it's possible that I'm ready,
    even if I don't feel like I am.

Choose Statement

I choose to feel my feelings,
hear my Safety Self,
and take my next step.

It's Not About
the Lessons

I've heard over and over that the point of life is to learn lessons and to grow. This implies that we're incomplete somehow because we need to grow and learn. It's the same right/wrong line of thought as "What am I doing wrong?"

The implication with the concept of lessons is that, once you learn something, you "pass" and don't have to have that lesson again. Until you get it right, you have to keep striving and trying.

I've even heard people say that the Universe is testing them. Does that sound like the actions of someone who fucking loves you?

Imagine a lover saying, "Darling, I love you more than I can ever say. Now, tell me my three favorite meals, and prove that you're worthy of my time, and I'll take you to dinner." Um, no.

And yet the idea of being tested feels like such a natural place to go when things happen! In the past three weeks, we've had one car and two major appliances die. In three weeks! I'll admit that, by the third one, I had a thought like, "*Is* this a test?!" The beauty of writing this book, though, is that I'm saying what I need to hear and remember. Because I'd recently been working on this chapter, it was fresh in my mind to open up to what this was bringing up, and to choose expansion.

At one of the Spiritual Retreats I did when I was working with Tapas, I was sitting with the deep question, "What is the purpose of life?" I was in a deep, meditative state when I asked the question. The response that popped into my mind was, "To live." I could almost feel the Divine eyeroll.

Talk about a lightning bolt of duh!

We're here to live, to experience the wonder of life. This isn't some kind of punitive school. It's life! We're here to explore, to connect, to love, to laugh, to play. And above all, we're here to experience the magic of who we are, the unique combination of humanity and divinity that exists nowhere else except the seat where you're sitting.

Certainly we learn things along the way, but that's not the point of life or our experiences. There is no final exam or graduation.

Another common misconception is that we're here to heal and that, to do this, we need to peel back the layers of our problem like the layers of an onion. Once you get to the core or the root of an issue, you heal it and then move on to another one.

Sounds fun, doesn't it?

As I discovered in my experience after Margaret

Alice's death, I was never broken. We don't need to heal. Any wounds we feel like we have are tender spots where we have unprocessed emotions and where we're holding old ways of seeing ourselves. It's where we're holding onto our S.T.U.F.F. Instead of peeling the layers to get to our "core wounding," I see us moving outward.

We are at the center of our lives. We are the core. Life invites us to expand outward. Expanding outward means that we live more fully. We live a bigger life. This doesn't have to mean that we have a bigger business, and it can mean that. It doesn't mean that we interact with more people, and it absolutely can mean that.

What it means is that we hold ourselves back less and less. We do more and more of what our soul longs for, with less and less doubt and uncertainty. Our life reflects who we truly are more and more, and we're more and more in harmony with the Universe.

Expansion Is the Key

The reason I say "more and more" and "less and less" is because it's not a goal we reach. There is no arrival place. We're always in the process of becoming.

We don't one day wake up and say, "OK, I'm totally me. There's no more room for my expansion." What would we do next, dissolve into the energy of the Universe?

OK, maybe that'll happen for some people someday. It's possible. Most of us have quite a bit of expanding to do first, though.

The image I have of this is that each of us is at the

53

center of our life, surrounded by rings. As we expand outward, we bump up against the next ring.

Every ring is made up of our S.T.U.F.F.—the thoughts, feelings, and fears that we've accumulated during our lives. It's important to know that this S.T.U.F.F. isn't something bad or evil. In fact, you accumulated the stuff for a very sound reason—it served you and kept you safe.

Think of a warm, cozy coat you wore as a young child. That coat protected you from the cold. It was what you needed at the time. Over the years, you've outgrown that coat. If you tried to put it on now, instead of feeling cozy and protective, it would feel constrictive and uncomfortable.

It's the same thing with your S.T.U.F.F. Growing up, you were dependent on others to keep you safe and to provide for your needs. You had to play by their rules. Regardless of how loving and attentive the adults in your life were, you were bound to have experiences where you felt isolated and alone. You learned what you had to do to get attention, to get what you felt you needed to survive, and, hopefully, to flourish.

Your fears protected you. Your thoughts guided you. You buried at least some of your feelings because that was the safer, easier way.

You are no longer that child.

The thoughts, fears, and feelings from those times are chafing. They feel constrictive. That's one of the reasons you're here reading this book.

It's so easy to look back with our adult eyes and judge our S.T.U.F.F. We resent having been in the position of believing it. We blame the adults in our lives. We fight against the S.T.U.F.F. But this is like judging that childhood coat. It should have been bigger. I shouldn't have needed it. It definitely should have been a better color and style.

That coat wasn't wrong. And there's nothing wrong with the fact that it doesn't fit you now. Growing up is the natural progression of life.

Your S.T.U.F.F. wasn't wrong. And there's nothing wrong with it not resonating with you now. Expansion is the natural process of living.

There's something else making up the rings around you—your identities. These old ways of seeing yourself as a child, parent, employee, business owner, INFP, ESTJ, Reiki master, coach, artist, class clown, rebel, peacemaker, or chef all have their place. It can be helpful and expansive to own some of these identities. And sometimes they become limiting and constrictive.

The process of expansion means we go beyond what we know ourselves to be. As we dissolve the S.T.U.F.F. and identities, the ring melts, and we have that much more space. We become that much bigger.

What would keep you from expanding through the rings? That's easy: Comfort.

The space you're currently occupying is your comfort zone. You know this space. It's cozy. You know who you are in this space. You're comfortable with the identities. You know where everything is and what to expect.

And guess what. You can stay here. Just like you are. For the rest of your life.

Sure, some parts of it aren't great. You might not like your job or your business. You might feel unfulfilled by your relationship. You might be distant from your family. But as they say, the devil you know is better than the devil you don't know.

And besides, you see how this works, right? You dissolve another ring and expand, and it's exciting and scary and new. Then, after a while, that's your new normal. And you get comfortable again. And then you're right back where you were, in your comfort zone, and you have to do it all over again. So why bother?

If you want to stay where you are, put down this book and go mostly enjoy your OK life. It's totally your choice.

But unless you're reading this book from some sort of obligation, that's not what your life is about. It isn't your highest calling.

You're here because you want to live a bigger, richer life. You want to be more alive.

You're Bigger Than You Think

Each time you dissolve a ring, you get more life, and your vibration increases. It's like a video game where you accomplish a feat and get more life units. Same idea, but what you get more of is *you*.

That's the real mind bender here. You aren't becoming someone different. You're simply letting go of what *isn't* you so that you embody and express more of who you already are. You're becoming more of you.

It's like all those rings are inside your body. Each time

you dissolve one, you inhabit more of your body. Except that instead of being inside your body, it's inside the essence of who you are. So, you expand into more of your true essence, the essence you've always already been.

I never told anyone this growing up because it seemed so weird, but there were times when, as a child, I would be lying in my bed with my eyes closed and I'd have this sense of being enormous. I literally couldn't feel my bed anymore and knew that, if I opened my eyes, I'd be way bigger than my room. I would have been able to pick my bed up with two fingers.

I never could bring myself to open my eyes. I had the thought that it would melt my brain and really freak me out, but I clearly remember that feeling of hugeness.

That's the feeling I get when I think of how big each of us truly and already is.

One other thing about your expansion: doing what brings you joy is the most effective way to expand. Because your expansion comes from embodying more of your essence, the things that are in alignment with that will feel light. You'll feel energized at the thought of them; excited. And they'll bring you joy.

This lightness and joyfulness doesn't mean that doing these things will be easy. Doing what expands you can feel very challenging at times. It makes sense that in addition to feeling excited when you think of something expansive, you may also feel nervous or even scared.

A few years ago, I participated in a ten-month intensive leadership program. You go through with the same group, going to four week-long retreats and working on projects and assignments together in between. I loved it and will be deeply connected with this group from now on.

At the same time, there were times when I had to dig deep and hold onto my commitment in order to keep showing up. Sometimes it was too hard, and I was too busy, and I just didn't want to. Well, part of me didn't. Choosing to stay in and go deeper led to some of the richest experiences of my life.

At one retreat, a person in the group mentioned having taken pole dancing classes. I was intrigued. It sounded like so much fun! Then my rational mind said, "She's younger than I am and in better shape. I don't have any business pole dancing!" My body and my heart, though, said, "YES!" So I signed up for classes.

There have been times during the pole classes when I've wanted to hide. Times when it seemed like every other person could do a move that I wasn't getting. A few months in, I signed on to be in a couple of group numbers for a student showcase. I had times of feeling like the weak link, the one people would look at and say, "Oh, well, at least she's trying."

And at the same time, I love it. I love how my body is getting strong and more flexible. I love how I'm showing up more in my life because of the energy and vibrancy I get from doing pole and chair dancing. I've even created a program where I teach women very basic chair dancing moves as a way to get in touch with their bodies and feelings, and to expand their comfort zones.

Things don't happen in our lives so that we learn lessons. We're given *opportunities* to *experience* ourselves in new ways. That's what takes our knowing of ourselves to deeper and deeper levels.

Mentally knowing that we're strong, courageous, powerful, loving, skillful, or anything else isn't the same as *experiencing* it. Each time we experience it, it becomes more deeply integrated and a part of our easy expression. When we're following what brings us joy, it's also a way of raising our vibration and increasing our aliveness.

Refuturing Statements

- ♥ What if it's possible that I'm not here to learn lessons.

- ♥ What if it's possible that the Universe really does love me and isn't testing me.

- ♥ What if it's possible that the Universe gives me opportunities to experience myself in new, stronger, and more expansive ways.

- ♥ What if it's possible that each time I take a step with intention and courage, I become stronger.

Choose Statement

I choose to be myself and claim
my power, one step at a time.

When the Shit
Hits the Fan

My client, Tara, was so excited on our first call. She was about to finalize a deal with someone that would move her business to the next level. We're talking a steady income, recognition, the whole shebang. She was over the moon.

Before our second call, her potential partner pulled out of the deal, and he wasn't even nice about it. In their conversation, he blamed Tara and made it sound like her fault that things fell apart.

Tara was tearful on that second call. She was living her worst nightmare. For a long time, she'd had a fear that she'd have a great opportunity and would sabotage it by not doing what she needed to do. She was always waiting for herself to do something wrong, and then beating herself up if it looked like she might have.

Talk about a big ring of S.T.U.F.F.

Listening to her, I could hear that while she *could* have bent over backwards to make him happy, the real issue was that he was asking her to do some unreasonable things as "her end" of the work. He wasn't respecting what she brought to the table, as though she needed to earn the right to work with him on something he wanted her to offer to his clients.

When we have a strong emotional reaction to something, like Tara was having to this, it's a signal that it's resonating with some old fears or beliefs we have about ourselves, or some unresolved experience from our past.

It's easy to label these experiences as bad, wrong, or shitty. We tend to get angry and resentful, moving into fight-or-flight mode. And we make it mean something about us. We're too scattered, not strong enough, or something else. We often feel like it confirms our worst fears about ourselves, like Tara was feeling.

Challenging experiences like this naturally bring up lots and lots of old S.T.U.F.F. It's one of their gifts. If you plough up a field, hidden rocks are brought up to the surface where they can be seen and removed, leaving the soil much more hospitable to new growth. Likewise, these situations stir up our buried S.T.U.F.F. so that we become aware of it and can release it.

Our emotional reaction is our signal that what's happening is resonating with our S.T.U.F.F. For instance, if someone told me that I'm too harsh and talk too much, I'd shrug it off. Like anyone, I can have my moments, but I'm far more likely to be the listener in a conversation and to speak gently, even when I'm giving direct feedback.

On the other hand, if someone said I wasn't blunt enough and didn't put myself into a conversation enough, it would sting. Depending on who said it, I might even feel hurt and angry. That's because those are areas where I've historically struggled. It would resonate with something I've feared about myself. I'm still working on knowing at a visceral level that I can fully speak up, so this is still a tender spot for me at times.

For Tara, what her potential partner said touched on old fears, especially around money. What I was able to help her see was that this was an *opportunity*. Just like ploughing brings up the existing rocks underneath the soil, those fears were already there. Her experiences of being betrayed and having men not show up for her were already a part of her past. This situation didn't *cause* her feelings as much as it *revealed* them.

Having them brought to the surface this way allowed her to *feel* those fears and release that old S.T.U.F.F. As we worked, old self-judgments and a huge weight of self-blame began dissolving. She let go of her identity of being someone who needed to be rescued by someone more powerful. Her attachments to her past experiences like this one melted away.

As she let the Refuturing Statements wash over her, she opened to new possibilities. She expanded into more confidence and self-reliance. She had inner space for greater creativity and vibrancy. She began trusting herself more and had a deeper sense of when someone wasn't going to be reliable or a good fit for her.

When we talked seven days later, Tara told me that she was actually glad she had gone through that experience. The new lightness and power that she felt was worth it!

And her business was benefitting. She was taking action on a great idea for a way to serve more clients and was ready to start letting go of relationships with people who drained her. She was getting more done, and it was coming from excitement rather than something she "should" do.

Breakdowns
Lead to Breakthroughs

Imagine what could happen if you see every breakdown as the start of a breakthrough. If you know that every shit show is S.T.U.F.F. getting cleaned off, and that, if you stick with it, if you let your old attachments and identities fall away, what will emerge will be a clearer, more powerful, and more congruent version of you.

When something "bad" happens, our response is typically to fight it, fix it, or flee it. It's so much more powerful to surrender to it and to use it for our own expansion.

I realize this isn't easy. I get that it goes against some deeply worn habits. I know that fighting, fixing, and fleeing are ways of feeling in control, of feeling safe. What if it's possible that being in control is actually a way of being stuck. What if it's possible that being in control is a euphemism for staying in your comfort zone. What if it's possible that surrendering is the way to release old S.T.U.F.F. and expand.

When I say surrender, I don't mean being passive. I simply mean accepting what is instead of fighting it.

When Tara first told me about the deal falling apart,

she clearly thought that this shouldn't have happened. If only she'd worked harder. If only she'd been a better person. If only she didn't need the money. Clearly, she was judging both the situation and herself as wrong.

When she began to see it as an opportunity for expansion, she stopped trying to fight, fix, or flee. Without that energy of struggle and resistance, it was so much easier for her to make changes. She was able to move into what I call the Three Cs. These are the steps to take in order to work through challenging situations in an expansive way.

First, feel your feelings. If you've got strong feelings going on, let them come up first. Not every challenging situation will be emotional, but if this one is, allow yourself to feel the emotions.

Step 1—Get Curious

Ask yourself questions like:

- If this situation is an opportunity, what might it be an opportunity *for*?

- If someone I've never met walked up and looked at what's going on, what would they see?

- Where is my power in this?

- How do I want to show up in this?

- What's important to me here?

Step 2—Get Creative

What creative possibilities can you come up with for this situation? Get ideas from your head, and also check in with your intuition and your heart. Crazy ideas are welcome! Impulses are too. Let yourself dream, like Tara did for her business.

Step 3—Get Courageous

Now it's time to move into action, and that takes courage. You're doing something new, so you'll naturally have some nervousness. You might even feel a little anxious or scared. You might dread taking the next step. That's OK. It's normal. What *else* do you feel?

Over and over I've heard clients say things like, "I'm excited about this opportunity, but I'm also really nervous. I don't know if I can do it." Using the word "but" is like putting on the brakes. Your excitement has your foot on the gas. Your "but" has you pushing the brake. It's really hard to make progress this way.

Try this instead. "I'm really nervous and have doubts, and I'm really excited about this opportunity." By acknowledging *all* of your feelings and using the word "and," you keep the momentum going forward. By addressing the fears and nervousness first, you let your Safety Self relax, and it's easier to move into more expansion.

Take a deep breath, and take one step at a time.

When you practice getting curious, creative, and courageous, you begin leading your life in a bigger way.

Typically, when something "bad" happens, we feel like a victim. We're at the mercy of fate, another person, or our own faults. Victims are weak and powerless, and that's how we end up feeling in our lives.

Not only are these situations opportunities, they're also catalysts.

When we approach them with curiosity, creativity, and courage, these experiences expand us. They're the stimulus that gets us into action and into more alignment with our essence and our joy.

Tara was catalyzed into creating ways of working with clients that truly excited her and ended up bringing her the income she was looking for. She was able to see that, had the deal not fallen through, she'd have been working with someone who didn't truly value her and who would have continued asking for more and more from her. That is *not* a recipe for feeling fulfilled and joyful.

If the situation you're dealing with is something cataclysmic, feeling your feelings can take a long time. It's not something to push yourself through. And you may cycle back through it numerous times.

When my daughter died, I grieved for a long time, of course. Over years and years, I would cycle through times of grief and layers of letting go of S.T.U.F.F. and my identities around the whole experience.

These steps are not intended to push you into action before you're ready or to deny your pain and sorrow. Sometimes, feeling your feelings is the most important step of all.

Refuturing Statements

♥ What if it's possible that it's OK for me
to feel my feelings.

♥ What if it's possible that I can do this in ways
that feel safe and right for me.

♥ What if it's possible that I can do this
at a time and at a pace that feels safe
and right for me.

♥ What if it's possible that I can feel nervous
and excited, scared *and* confident,
even exhilarated.

♥ What if it's possible that I have more options
and possibilities than I ever realized.

♥ What if it's possible for me to be curious,
creative, and courageous as I become
the leader of my life.

Choose Statement

I choose to get curious, creative,
and courageous as I take
inspired action.

Shit's Getting Real

I'm sitting here in a cabin writing this book and it's happened. I've hit a block.

I try for a while to force myself to write. I push. I have a fear sometimes that I don't push myself enough. Sometimes I look at others, and it looks like they accomplish so much more than I do. For instance, I was supposed to meet a friend on my way home Friday, and she texted that she's behind on some stuff and can't get together. I make that mean that she's busy, that she's got more going on than I do, and that she's making stuff happen and I'm not.

From there I spiral into, "I haven't heard back from my editor. What if she doesn't like what I've written so far?" Now, keep in mind that she hadn't asked me to send anything to her yet, and that I had because, well, let's be honest here, I want a pat on the back. At the same time, I know that if she said anything, good or bad, I'd be tempted to get caught up in that, and my job right now is simply to write. Editing comes later. AND, she did let me know that she probably wouldn't be able to look at the pages until tonight or tomorrow, so what do I expect?

After a little while, I pull myself together and remember what I know to do. I close my computer, put one hand on top of the other over my heart chakra, and let my mind spin until I get to the feelings. Now, I just feel. Thoughts spin through my head. Then I feel a wave of shame and guilt. It gets more intense, and then it passes.

Now an urge to share this with you comes up, quickly followed by fear.

> *Heck, you're reading the book I'm writing!*
> *What if you get disgusted, thinking I was more*
> *together than this, and put it down?*

And then the thought comes up: "I can't control that. I can only be me. Some readers *might* get disgusted and put the book down." OK, that's their choice. That's about where they are and what's right for them, and their needs and preferences.

Other people might read this and think, "Thank goodness. It's not just me." Or even, "Oh, I get it now. *That's* how I can handle these situations."

Now I feel a wave of love and compassion, for myself and for all of us. We ALL get stuck and "in our stuff" sometimes. We all have areas of stretch and expansion. OK, right now this one is mine.

Now a wave of pride comes up.

> *I'm writing a book! I've never done this before.*

Just a few months ago, I was dreaming of having time away to write, and of having someone to help me think it all through, who really believes in what I'm creating and has the expertise about editing and publishing that I don't. And now, here I am, in a cabin, with an editor who is all of that and more, and the support of my family and friends.

I'm really proud of myself for going this deep into what I believe and teach, of wading through when it felt like I had so much to say that it was like I was trying to pour a bucket of water through a straw.

I'm proud that I'm doing this retreat like I want all of my life to be, to have energy flowing, and to have times of rest and times of inspired activity. I'm proud of honoring all that I've learned about myself and how I work best, and of having built the capacity to hold the incredibly strong energy I'm feeling as I do this.

I'm proud of letting you into my experience, of showing up authentically. I'm proud to continue living what I teach, modeling and giving permission for other people to be imperfect. I'm proud of continuing to pole dance, and the practice it gives me in showing up imperfectly!

My mother tells the story of the first steps I took. After practicing by holding onto the fur of the poodle who lived next door (thanks, Sammy), for my first solo steps I went down the sidewalk, up the driveway, up a couple of steps, and into the house. She doesn't know where I went from there.

Clearly, my desire to look good, to not show my stumbles and wobbles, started early. So I'm deeply proud that I do so much imperfectly now. And I freaking love that I'm willing to be awkward and inept. It's opening up so much for me to learn and explore, and I'm having so much fun doing it.

This process of writing, of creating something this big, of being so aligned with who I am, is changing me. Or rather, it's changing how I show up for myself and my work.

We're all recovering from something—from being a perfectionist, a worrier, a hider, an avoider, a victim, a pusher, a settler. We can be real about our struggles and challenges, or we can keep up our façades.

Giving up the façades means letting ourselves be broken open. Sometimes it's going to look like a breakdown—when a relationship ends, a job doesn't work out, a client leaves, a loved one betrays us, or when we mess up something really big. The problem isn't the breakdown.

The breakdown is needed as a course correction. Something is out of alignment, and we've gotten off track. Our course needs to be corrected to come more into alignment with our essence.

This is what happens for me when I get stuck with my writing. I feel blocked because I'm too in my head.

Getting stuck is my mini-breakdown. When I feel out of my power, I want someone to rescue me, like my editor or a friend.

Reclaiming my power means stopping, getting quiet, and going inside. It's uncomfortable sitting with some of those thoughts and feelings, and it felt super uncomfortable sharing it with you as I wrote the first part of this chapter.

The payoff is that doing this has cleared the way for my heart and my spirit to speak. It cleared the way for authenticity instead of continuing to push in the hopes of looking good. I have energy, joy, and a sense of spaciousness that I didn't 15 minutes ago.

My goal isn't not to stumble. If I'm not stumbling, I'm continuing to walk the same safe path that I'm comfortable with. Trying something new and going beyond my comfort zone includes stumbling. Sometimes I feel like the weak link, the worst one in the class. Sometimes I may be. But it means I'm exploring and expanding.

There's a popular quote that says, "If you're the smartest person in the room, you're in the wrong room." When I keep putting myself in situations where I'm not the best, as uncomfortable and embarrassing as it can feel, I live a fuller and richer life.

I'm going to take a break now and eat and then do some chair dancing. And then I'll be back. I'm choosing to keep showing up, for myself and for you, and I'll do it in a way that's real for me.

Doing what scares me, breaking open, letting go—

this is where the juiciness of life is. It's how I reclaim more and more of my power.

One last confession before I go, I have a new addiction. I look for ways to get into my discomfort zone, because the payoff is oh, so sweet in the long run.

Refuturing Statements

♥   What if it's possible that it's OK for me
to honest with myself.

♥   What if it's possible that everyone hits
blocks and challenges at times.

♥   What if it's possible that this is part
of the process of expansion.

♥   What if it's possible that the more aware
I am of my thoughts and feelings,
the more easily and quickly they dissolve.

Choose Statement

I choose to be gentle with myself
as I do what feels uncomfortable.

Co-creating
with the Universe

Recently, I saw a post on Facebook saying the author isn't a fan of "letting the Universe lead." Instead, she said, she prefers "living awake" and listening deeply to her heart and its whispers.

With all respect to the wise woman who wrote that, letting the Universe lead and listening to the whispers of your soul are the same thing.

In December 2011, while I was still working for Tapas, I attended an event led by Christine Kane, founder of Uplevel You. I was amazed to find a business coach who knew all about strategy and who also really got energy. She even used some of the same concepts that we'd taught in the TAT workshops!

Even though I'd never invested so much money in myself before, I signed up to work with her for a year. Six months later, Christine called me and asked if I wanted to be her first ever associate coach and do my work with all of her clients. She'd seen how the fears and self-doubt kept clients from implementing the strategies she was teaching them and knew that they needed energy/ mindset work.

For five years I worked with Christine, her team, and the clients. Other associate coaches were added on and it was great to be part of this company as I continued to build my own business. In fact, I loved this work so much that I wondered how I would one day make the decision to go.

Many people might say "going with the flow" would have meant staying in that position, doing what I'd gotten masterful at doing, and waiting for a sign from the Universe that it was time to change. A sign to them might be a big argument, or maybe getting so unhappy about something that I couldn't stand it anymore, or being let go by the company. None of that would have been OK with me because it would have been out of integrity for me and out of alignment with my love and respect for everyone involved.

Instead, I listened to my inner guidance.

At the last event I attended, my body and my heart gave me clear signals that it was time for me to go. The clearest was when I was standing on stage, looking at this room full of amazing business owners, and had a thought so loud that it was like someone said it in my head: "I have far more to teach than I can do from here. It's time for me to find my own stage."

This was the Universe (aka my inner guidance) nudging me, showing me my next move via my feelings and thoughts. Being awake and courageous allowed me to hear and act on it.

In contrast, I was in another situation once where I

knew it was time to leave, and I didn't. I was afraid of losing the job, the connections, and the status it gave me. Eventually, the decision was taken out of my hands, as my responsibilities were given to others and I literally had nothing to do.

Often, when people say they let the Universe lead, they mean that they wait until something dramatic happens, like getting get fired from a job or having their spouse leave them.

The Universe first guides us much more subtly than that. Some people hear it best through their desires or the soft whispers of their souls. Some people have an inner GPS (often in the stomach or heart) that guides them via physical sensations. For some, it's just a knowing or hearing guidance being spoken inside them. Some people get it through dreams.

When we don't hear (or don't act on) the early messages, the delivery gets more dramatic. You didn't hear the whisper to leave the job that wasn't right for you? OK, how about if you get fired? Outer signs are often the Universe ramping up the intensity so you'll take action.

Sometimes when something "bad" happens—a job ends, a spouse leaves, money troubles abound, or sickness comes—we think, at least in part, that we're being punished. And the regrets start. If only I'd done better, made different choices, or was a better person, this wouldn't have happened. We think that the Universe is making us pay up.

That's not how the Universe, who fucking loves us, works.

Most often, we've been getting inner signals that something's off. We feel an urge to look for a new job, or to leave a relationship, or to take better care of our health, but we're scared. Staying comfortably miserable can seem much more appealing than going into our discomfort zone and seeking out change because we get scared.

But our soul longs for more. Our soul wants the full experience of life, so when we don't follow the gentle nudges of the Universe, the Universe lovingly turns up the heat. When you listen for the whispers, increasing the intensity isn't needed.

Our #1 job is to show up, to be awake, and to take action when it's called for. If we don't, it's as though we're just standing still. Picture a couple on the dance floor with one person leading and the other standing still. The leader has to stop dancing and focus on simply getting the partner to take one little step. With a single step, the dance can begin again.

The Universe needs / wants / expects you to dance along. Otherwise, what's the point?

The more fit and flexible you are and the more you've honed your skills, the more elaborate and fun a dance the Universe can lead you in. You have to sit down and do the work. You have to show up. Be awake, alert, responsive, and determined.

A dance teacher told me once that I was being too flexible, that I needed to tighten my muscles so that he had something to push against. He wasn't encouraging struggle or resistance, but rather being grounded and strong in myself so that I was meeting him in the dance. The

Universe wants the same thing. It wants us to meet it in the dance.

Where I disagree with my friend's post on Facebook is that I don't think that our soul's whispers are us telling the Universe what to do. It's more co-creative than that. There's a flow that, when we're clear and free, allows the dance to unfold.

The Universe speaks to us through our wants and the whispers of our souls. Our saying yes to our soul-level wants signals that we're ready, we're in, and we're prepared to dance.

The three keys to dancing with the Universe are:

- **Listen**—Have times of quiet when you're deeply in touch with your own thoughts and feelings. Pay attention. What are your body and heart telling you?

- **Trust**—Trust yourself and the Universe. Don't try to figure everything out or force things to happen. Trusting allows you to relax, hear, and be guided. You have to be relaxed in order to dance well and be open to receive.

- **Show Up**—Dare to know. Dare to be clear. Dare to act on your clarity. Say yes. Step up. Jump off.

Letting go of what's weighing you down and holding you back greatly increases your ability to listen, trust, and show up. While you can do them even when you're stressed, overwhelmed, and feeling stuck, you won't feel the same sense of ease and grace.

This isn't about pushing. It's about letting go and stepping up.

Refuturing Statements

♥ What if it's possible that I have intuition and inner guidance.

♥ What if it's possible for me to know and understand what my inner guidance is telling me.

♥ What if it's possible for me to trust my inner guidance.

♥ What if it's possible that my inner guidance is getting clearer and more understandable every day.

♥ What if it's possible for me to listen, trust and show up.

Choose Statement

I choose to be open to my inner guidance and to act on its messages.

Power

If you want to find out who the richest person in the world is, all you have to do is Google it. Money is such a measurable substance. That's one reason we use it so often to measure ourselves and others. It's an easy way to keep score.

It's also fairly objective. No one's going to argue that $1,000 is more than $1,000,000. Of course, factoring in different currencies and valuations of possessions can get hairy, and still, there are ways of handling that.

But when you talk about power, it's a whole different story.

Is the most powerful person in the world the one with the most firepower? The most resources? How about the one who can motivate the most people to create change?

One reason "power" is hard to measure is that there are different types of power.

The type most people think of when you say "power" is "power over." Power over has created much of the way the world is now. Power over led to colonialism and the slave trade. It led to hierarchical structures in governments, schools, some religions, and homes.

The United States was created as a republic with lots of checks and balances in an effort to mitigate power over.

Power over is an "us vs. them," "winner and loser," "aggressor and victim" type of power. It's competitive. You know you're strong because someone else is weak. Because of this, only a limited number of people can be powerful, so everyone fights to be the one who wins. In fact, with power over, you *can't* be strong unless someone else is weak, so you benefit from others' weaknesses.

Look to any conqueror, dictator, or authoritarian leader, and you'll see examples of power over. Based in fear, many brutal acts have been committed in the quest for power over. Insults and derogatory name-calling are also bids for power over.

People who are focused on power over are always trying to get something—money, compliance, approval, a sense of safety. They also take up more than their share of resources, space, and conversation—sometimes it even feels like they try to take up the most oxygen in a room. Their energy is focused outward, worrying about what other people do, say, and think.

The other type of power is power from within.

This is the power of leaders like Jesus, Buddha, Gandhi, Mother Teresa, and Martin Luther King, Jr. When you're powerful in this way, everyone benefits: your loved ones, your clients, your community. In other words, everyone wins.

With this type of power, you're powerful whether you're sitting alone or leading a group of thousands. Power from within comes from knowing and being yourself and is more a way of being than anything else. It lights you up from inside and gives you a sense of your own self-worth. At the same time, people with inner power are humble, honoring the inner power of others, with no need to prove anything to themselves or anyone else.

The single biggest difference in the two types of power is that power over is something you acquire or are given. Power from within is something you already have. The challenge is in accessing and claiming it.

To own your inner power is to own all of who you are. Deep honesty, most especially honesty with yourself, is non-negotiable. You can't live your truth while pretending that things are OK when they're not, while not standing up for your beliefs, or while not taking action on your dreams. This means that owning your power often requires you to go outside your comfort zone.

What's really interesting about these two types of power is that you can go back and forth between the two. I've seen this a lot in my parenting. There are times when it's been necessary to exert my power over ("play the mom card"), like when someone's well-being was in question. At other times, I've done it because I didn't know what else to do, got scared, fell into old habits, or mimicked what "everyone else" was doing. Those times didn't work out nearly as well as the ones when I came from my own power and collaborated with my kids to find something that worked for all of us.

This is true for every single relationship, not just with kids. There may be areas of your life where you're focused on power from within, and others where you're focused on power over. I've walked away from conversations realizing that I was participating in a power struggle, trying to prove myself right and the other person wrong, rather than seeking to hear and work together.

When you're connected with your power, you're *creating* your life rather than living by reaction or default. You're being a leader of yourself and your life, which is the very definition of power from within.

Everything I've been talking to you about in this book leads to your owning your inner power more and more. Again, I say "more and more" because owning your power is a process. With a commitment to awareness, support, and guidance, you can make a conscious choice about which type of power dynamic you participate in at each moment.

Owning your power means owning your brilliance. Marianne Williamson nailed it when she said the following, which I'm going to quote in its entirety here. Even if you've read it a thousand times, I encourage you to read it again.

Our deepest fear is not that we are inadequate. Our deepest fear is that we are powerful beyond measure. It is our light, not our darkness, that most frightens us. We ask ourselves, Who am I to be brilliant, gorgeous, talented, fabulous? Actually, who are you not to be? You are a child of God. You playing small does not serve the world. There is nothing enlightened about shrinking so that other people won't feel insecure around

you. We are all meant to shine, as children do.
We were born to make manifest the glory of God
that is within us. It's not just in some of us; it's in
everyone. And as we let our own light shine, we
unconsciously give other people permission to do
the same. As we are liberated from our own fear,
our presence automatically liberates others.

When I read this, I imagine each of us as a piece of glass in a stained-glass mosaic window. Our job isn't to try to take over the window, or to convince the other pieces of glass to become the same color we are. Nor is it helpful to try to turn ourselves into the same color as the pieces around us.

Our job is to be the piece of glass that we were created to be so that the image as a whole is complete.

Our job is to continually let go of anything that clouds our clarity so that the light shines brightly through us.

Our job is to completely fill our proper space. Shrinking so that there are gaps around us detracts from the overall effect, and encourages other pieces to do the same.

Our job is to embrace all the facets of who we are so that we have as much richness and depth of color as possible.

The color and hue of the glass that you are matters. The shape matters. And still, no shape or hue is better than any other. No shape or hue is right or wrong. The full image would be incomplete if any piece were missing or changed. Each is incredibly special, and none is better than any other.

It doesn't matter what brings you life and joy. Whether it's being a coach, a musician, an activist, a leader in the world, your community, or your family, it doesn't matter.

What matters is that you be vibrant and joyful. When you're living your truth, life works for you, and life works as a whole. You don't have to know the grand plan for your life in order to live it and love it. Keep exploring. Keep expanding. Keep taking steps.

Some people won't appreciate you and your gifts and your truth. In some ways, it's like you're speaking Swahili, and they're speaking Greek. There's nothing wrong, it's simply that you're speaking two different languages.

Of course, some people won't see it this way. They believe that their language is the right one. They'll deny the validity of yours and will insist that you learn and speak theirs. They're going for power over. Then you have a choice to make.

Do you get angry and argue for the rightness of your language? Or competitive and try to make them understand why *yours* is better?

Do you give up yours and speak only theirs?

Do you leave them to speak their language and go to find the people who speak your language, or who are willing to learn yours and teach you theirs?

It can be lonely if you don't know others who speak your language. One of the best things about the internet is that you can find other speakers and connect with them, even if they're scattered across the globe. The main thing you have to do is to search and let them know that you're there and want to talk.

Whatever it looks like to be you, show up as that. The rest of us need you, as you, to make the picture complete.

Refuturing Statements

♥ What if it's possible that I don't need to control others or situations in order to be safe and happy.

♥ What if it's possible that living my truth is the path to my power.

♥ What if it's possible I am unique and beautiful, just as I am.

♥ What if it's possible that there's something special about me and that I fill a space that no one else can.

♥ What if it's possible that everyone benefits when I take up my rightful space.

♥ What if it's possible that everyone benefits when I let myself shine.

Choose Statement

I choose
to let myself
shine.

Armor Down

When I got my first apartment, my roommate and I went furniture shopping at a flea market. I was so proud of myself when I found a dresser that I liked and that was in my price range.

Over time, my pride turned into frustration.

Every time the dresser got bumped during a move, a piece of the finish chipped off. I was moving at least once a year, and doing it with the help of friends, mostly just stuffing as much as we could into our cars. Bumps were inevitable.

Several years and multiple moves later, my nice dresser was looking pretty ratty. The problem was that my dresser was only nice on the outside. It was made out of cheap wood covered by a thin layer of nice wood. This is a common practice known as veneer. As long as it's left undisturbed, it looks great. But that was not the life of a dresser in my household at that time.

I thought of that dresser at the first retreat for the leadership program I did. I shared with everyone my realization that I'd always had a veneer of "I'm fine." I used "I'm fine" to cover up any number of hurts and pains, especially the times when I felt less than.

At one point I said, "No matter what happened, I'd take it in and then hide behind, 'I'm fine'. My daughter was in the hospital for seven weeks as a newborn, and 'I'm fine.' My next baby died, and 'I'm fine.'"

One of the leaders looked at me with great compassion and said, "It breaks my heart that you can say the words, 'My baby died, and I'm fine.'"

In that moment, a dam inside me broke. A wail like I've never uttered in my life rose out of me. I was no longer conscious of being in that room or with those people. I was awash in pain I'd buried for a very long time. It wasn't just my pain for Margaret Alice's death, but hurt and pain that I'd carried all my life.

Opening my eyes to see those 27 near-strangers surrounding me, holding me, staying present with me as tears and snot ran down my face was transforming. Here I was, the least "OK" I'd ever let myself be, and they hadn't run away screaming. I was raw and real, and they were still there. Not only did I shatter, I did it in full view of everyone.

If I could give every person in the world a gift, it would be to have the experience of letting yourself be totally raw and real while being seen and held.

This experience was a quantum leap in my ability to show up and be myself. This group has given me the *experience* of being seen and loved time and again. It's been close to three years since that first retreat, and we continue to lovingly and fiercely push each other to show up more, give more, and be more of who we are.

Before this, I knew on a mind and somewhat on a heart

and body level that any "seeming" we hold onto, not only holds others away, it holds us in. Breaking open in front of everyone helped me get it in a much more cellular way.

I still work to experience the power of my authenticity in every area of my life. I want to know the freedom of being fully myself like I know that ice is cold. I want it to be something that comes as naturally as breathing and doesn't require a second thought.

I've heard the same desire from clients over and over. We all want to be seen and loved for who we are. At the same time, we work hard to conform, to fit in, and to not have flaws. We cover ourselves with a beautiful veneer and don't even realize we're doing it.

It's not that we're trying to deceive anyone. I thought that being fine was what I was *supposed* to do. I thought that meant I was "handling things well," "doing my work," and "putting my best foot forward." The problem was that I wasn't being fully honest with myself about how I felt, and what I wanted and needed. I thought that being self-sufficient was the goal, and that to do that, I had to be fine. In fact, I had no idea how "not fine" I was at some level!

Being "fine" served me well for a long time. It helped me get where I was. It helped me get through some really difficult times in my life. It gave me the space I needed to learn new tools, to have other experiences, and to serve lots of clients. And in many, many ways, I *was* fine. I was not a broken person. I could have gone the rest of my life like this and been OK.

Except that being OK isn't enough. Fine isn't enough.

I'm dedicated to living the highest version of myself that I can, so I couldn't stay forever with that little part of me feeling hurt and disconnected. It wasn't expressing my true essence, and that made a difference overall.

It got to be like the princess and the pea. That not-fine-ness was making me more and more uncomfortable. That part of me was out of resonance with the rest of me. As my energy got more and more clear and I got stronger and stronger, the contrast became greater and greater. And like a high-pitched squeal on an otherwise crystal-clear phone call, it got more and more annoying.

Even if other people weren't aware of it, I knew that there was something holding me back, something that wasn't fully aligned and authentic. The reason I signed up for the leadership program in the first place was because I wanted to be more *me*!

The great irony, of course, is that in allowing myself to be "not fine" and letting the group see me at my most vulnerable moment, all that "not fine" S.T.U.F.F. dissolved. It had to because *it wasn't the truth of who I am*. It was the truth of how I was feeling and the identities I'd been holding onto. It wasn't *who* I am.

Unlike my dresser, there was something very valuable underneath the veneer and cheap wood.

Underneath our veneer and our S.T.U.F.F. is the truth of who we are, our real essence. Our essence is made of the material of the Universe, and that's love. Remember the image of the glass mosaic? Each of us, underneath the dust and veneer and crap, is a beautiful piece of glass, with a specific shape and color, that's designed to shine the light of the Universe. Having a veneer over the glass makes it opaque and dark because the light can't get through.

I describe this with my clients as putting icing over shit. The icing doesn't change the shit, it just covers it up for a while. Isn't it better to wash off the shit and reveal the treasures beneath? *This* is the path to true freedom.

Stretching

At our most recent leadership retreat, we gave each other two stretch words. These were things that the group wants to see more of from each person and that would expand the person's range of expression. Some of the stretch words were: *messy, subtle, scary, innocent, cocky, playful, still, wise, velvety,* and *authority.* We knew we'd hit on the "right" words for someone when they squirmed with discomfort.

My two words were *bold* and *awkward*, and squirm I did!

Bold I could get, but they wanted me to be more *awkward? Really?!?* Isn't awkward one of those things that it's better *not* to be??

Through exercises at the retreat, I began pushing myself to be bold and awkward. This meant doing things I wasn't comfortable with and wasn't sure I could do well. It meant going into my discomfort zone and doing things I felt unsure of. In front of people. And the lightbulb came on. I worked to always be graceful and fluid—and that was part of my veneer, part of my identity.

Sometimes the exercises turned out really well and

93

everything went smoothly. Sometimes I was really awkward, and I *survived*! I usually laughed as much as anyone else.

Finally I got that embracing awkward doesn't mean I have to *be* awkward. It means being *willing* to be awkward. It means being OK with the risk, knowing that being awkward won't kill me. It means being willing to have my imperfections seen.

My veneer was a combination of "I'm fine" and gracefulness. I've known people whose veneer was "fierceness," "humor," "talking," "listening," "niceness," "apathy," "controlling," "being organized," "being flighty".... Every one of these is an asset when it's authentic. Often, I truly *am* happy and graceful. It's when we feel like we *have* to be these things that they become limiting. That's when they become a veneer.

Once I was willing to risk being seen as awkward, I discovered that I knew more and could do more than I'd realized. I began stretching my wings in a whole new way, and it feels amazing! I'm being myself more and following my soul's lead to do what's mine to do.

The biggest surprise of letting go of my veneer, though, is how much more I can *receive*!

My veneer not only kept me *in*, it also kept others *out*. Even when I got compliments, they couldn't fully penetrate the veneer and the S.T.U.F.F., so I never fully felt them. It was like I had a hole that couldn't seem to be filled.

Jealousy was a sign of my inner sense of lack. Here's an example.

I used to feel jealous when other people were praised.

It wasn't the only thing I felt, of course. I also felt excited for them, proud of them, etc. And, in the background, there was a little voice saying things like, "Why don't they say these things about me? Don't they know I'm awesome too? Why don't they see me?"

The problem wasn't that people weren't willing or trying to see me. The problem was that I wasn't fully showing myself, so they couldn't. Plus, I wasn't fully taking in what they said when they *could* see me. No wonder that little, hidden part of me never felt full! It never was!

In those areas where I was focused on appearing fine when I wasn't, I wasn't seeing *myself.* I was trying to hide what I saw as my weaknesses, my weirdness, and my imperfection. I couldn't see the beauty and strength of those parts of me, so I hid them away.

I knew this had all changed when, one day, we were celebrating a birthday in our leadership group in a group chat we have. I realized that I was reading each new post for this person with pure love and delight. With each acknowledgement and every word of praise for this person, I felt lighter and more joyful.

Then it happened again with the next birthday celebration soon after that. To see if this change was real, I went and read Facebook posts from people I used to compare myself to. I didn't feel jealous!

This wasn't a case of having good days or reading praise of someone I felt especially close to. This was a deep down, fundamental change.

What a sense of freedom and joy! What a sense of openness. As we get more and more full from the inside

95

out, we need less and less recognition from others. And ironically, as we relax and lose the energy of *needing* recognition, we're more likely to get it. The energy of needing and grasping is repelling, not magnetic.

Recently, when my husband offered to address a challenging situation for me, I had an old impulse to say, "It's OK, I'll do it." In that moment, I was able to stop myself and say instead, "Thanks. That would be great."

I didn't accept his help because I was weak or because I was avoiding doing it myself. Just the opposite. I knew I could do it, and so I didn't have to. For many reasons, he's actually the better person to do it, so why not let go and let him?

I don't need to block that flow in order to prove anything.

When Veneer Becomes Armor

We want so badly to receive things like love, abundance, recognition, and help. The problem is that we also want to protect ourselves, which we do by creating veneer. When veneer is really, really thick, it becomes armor.

Armor is so dense that even less gets in or out. It can be made of the same things that veneer is, like looking good, control, fierceness, niceness, and humor. Money, a toned body, intelligence, and possessions can also serve as armor, as can an addiction to alcohol, sex, gambling, or worry. Armor is anything you use to create a buffer between you and the world, or between you and your feelings.

Armor is like wearing Wonder Woman's bracelets

nonstop. Not only are bullets and arrows knocked away, but so are compliments, feedback, offers of help, and others' vulnerability. On the inside, feelings, fears, and anything that's perceived to be weak or negative gets blocked with amazing speed.

This isn't wrong or bad.

Just like my "I'm fine" veneer served me, armor serves the wearer. People who have armor have *needed* armor. They are people who've had big challenges in life. In many cases, when they were children, the adults whose job it was to protect and nurture them were the ones who hurt them the most. The armor kept them safe. In some cases, it even kept them alive.

Sometimes the armor comes from later experiences. I've had the honor of working with combat veterans, including someone from the military's elite mission unit, Delta Force. The emotional and psychological armor they developed helped them survive some horrific scenarios. It brought them home. Later though, it kept them from reconnecting with their families and reintegrating into civilian life.

That's the problem with armor. While it does a great job of protecting, it also does a great job of separating, leaving the wearer feeling lonely and isolated. It also keeps you from relaxing and breathing deeply.

The great news is that your armor isn't who you are. This means that it can be released. As you dissolve the S.T.U.F.F. that's holding it in place and making it feel safe and comfortable, it'll begin to loosen and let go. And you get to do this in the way and at the time that's right for you. There's no need to rip it off before you're ready.

The biggest thing I'd suggest is not to fight the armor. Just like your Safety Self, your armor is trying to protect you. Fighting it only holds it in place more tightly. Instead of judging and resisting it, look back and see how it's served you. See what outdated thoughts and beliefs are still hanging around, and let them go.

The other thing I'd say is, if this has been a big issue for you, get help. Just being seen and held in my vulnerability made a huge difference for me. Working with someone who sees you in ways you can't yet see yourself and who can be with your pain is transformational. They'll also be able to see your gifts and brilliance in ways that you can't yet. If you've been in situations that seemed life-threatening, I strongly encourage working with someone who's very skilled in this work.

A word about the following Refuturing Statements: If you have significant armor, these may not feel true to you for quite some time. A client told me that hearing me say, "What if it's possible that I'm safe and OK, just as I am" seemed to bounce off her. Even after listening multiple times to the recording I made for her, she simply couldn't take it in.

Then on one of our calls, she experienced a really big release. She cried tears that had been held in for many, many years, and a big batch of S.T.U.F.F. dissolved. After that, she was able to hear the statement in a whole new way and actually take it in.

The thing is that, even when it felt like the words were

bouncing off, her listening to those recordings again and again helped soften the ground for her big breakthrough. That happens. Energy work can sometimes feel like it's not doing anything because you don't feel or see changes right away. Then all of a sudden, boom! Something big shifts. Or you realize that you're "suddenly" doing something with ease when it used to be a big challenge for you.

If these statements don't feel like they're soaking in, that's OK. Hold them lightly and with the thought, "What if it's possible." You can even make them questions if that feels better for you.

Refuturing Statements

- ♥ What if it's possible that I'm safe and OK, just as I am.

- ♥ What if it's possible that that's true, even if it doesn't always feel true, or didn't feel true in the past.

- ♥ What if it's possible that being who I am is safe for me.

- ♥ What if it's possible that I know when I can be fully myself, and when I don't need to share or show all of me.

- ♥ What if it's possible that I'm not broken.

- ♥ What if it's possible that I'm OK and safe, just as I am.

Choose Statement

I choose to have fun
and be myself.

When You're About to Pop

Miriam was in her 70s when she came to see me, and my heart hurt just looking at her. Even though this was probably 10 years ago, I can still see her clearly in my mind.

Miriam wasn't disfigured in any way and didn't have any obvious injuries. I had just never seen anyone as tense as she was. Her smile, if you can call it that, was a tight line across her face, and I could see that her jaw was clenched. Her eyes seemed to hardly move in their sockets, and her entire body was rigid.

For months, Miriam had been plagued by a whooshing sound in her ears. It started at the same time every evening and would be gone when she woke up the next morning. It consumed her when it was happening, and the dread of its coming hung over her every day.

Multiple doctors, including some at the Mayo clinic, had checked her heart, arteries, hearing, and everything they could think of. Not one had been able to find a cause for the tinnitus.

When I asked Miriam what it was like, she described it as a roaring sound that filled her brain.

As she and I talked, she mentioned her parents a few times. They had been very important in her life, and she loved them deeply. She still thought of them often, though they'd both been dead for years. In fact, the conversation around her parents had the most charge to it, so to my surprise, that's where we focused our work rather than on the tinnitus.

Miriam and her husband were very well off financially and had recently had a big increase in their income. She lived a life of ease and comfort, while her parents had worked hard their entire lives.

As I guided her into her feelings, Mariam discovered a profound sense of guilt, as though she were betraying her parents by having such abundance. It didn't seem right that she should have things so easy when they'd struggled so much. Her wracking sobs came from such a deep place that I knew something big was shifting.

Once she'd cried her tears, it was like I was watching the sun come out after a rain. From somewhere even deeper than the tears came the sure knowing that her parents were happy for her, that her joy brought them joy. She realized how much she'd closed down because her life seemed too good.

Miriam's physical transformation was breathtaking. Her eyes sparkled, she laughed, and a genuine smile spread across her face. Her shoulders lowered as her body relaxed. Miriam's grace and flow were restored, and peace radiated from her. The woman sitting in front of me was not the same woman who'd shuffled in. This woman looked ready to dance.

In shutting down her feelings, Miriam had shut down her radiance and flow. She'd become rigid, not just emotionally, but physically as well. Her tinnitus was a result of this. When her feelings and energy were released, the tinnitus disappeared. I got an email several weeks later saying that it hadn't come back, and she was enjoying her life again.

The original Miriam reminded me of my yard when we'd been having a drought for a couple of years. We had been praying for rain for months, and when it finally came, the ground was so hard it couldn't receive it. The water simply ran off, not reaching even a half-inch down into the soil.

When we become that impenetrable, we simply aren't open to receiving.

I had another client, Ellie, who'd undertaken a huge project. She felt like the responsibility of it was all on her, and it was a tremendous weight. She wondered if she'd taken on too much and overcommitted herself. She felt guilty because of the strain on her marriage and family, and she was constantly beating herself up.

When she told me about people who'd offered to help her, there was a sense of guilt. Her energy around it was, "I've messed this up so much that people feel sorry for me. I feel bad that they're having to do this, and I can't possibly do it by myself." Checking in with her body, she felt a weight on her shoulders and a deadness in her arms.

As we worked and I helped Ellie recognize and release these emotions, she began radiating a different energy. She began to see her life through a new lens, taking in how much she enjoyed the people she was working with on the project, and how much *they* enjoyed being with *her*. The more she softened, the more deeply she could *feel* the appreciation and connection that had been around her the whole time. Again, it was like watching the sun coming out.

Both Miriam and Ellie had been so filled with their own guilt, shame, and self-criticism that there wasn't room for anything else. And it made them very "triggery!" Something that they normally could handle would just do them in. They were like balloons that had been over-inflated and stretched too thin. It didn't take much at all to pop them.

Once they'd released their emotions and thoughts, especially all the "shoulds" they'd been telling themselves, they became much softer. It took a great deal more to make them pop then!

When we're feeling as full and weighed down as these women were, we tend to think that we either need to work harder, or we need numb out. Or we flip-flop between the two.

What makes the difference, though, is tuning in to what's really going on. For some people, that happens while writing creatively or in a journal. For others, meditating makes that connection, or hiking while being present to nature and themselves. The key is to increase the level of your inner awareness, so you can recognize and release the S.T.U.F.F. that's been filling you up.

By acknowledging our thoughts and feeling our feelings, we deflate our balloon and let ourselves soften. We also increase our capacity to receive the abundance that's already around us, and to connect with our own creativity, flow, and joy.

On our next call, Ellie told me that she'd been challenged by an illness and some technological issues. At the same time, she'd made *huge* progress on her project—with the help of several other people—and had been taking better care of herself than she had in a very long time. It was only a few minutes into our call before she was relaxing and radiating out the joy she'd rediscovered the week before. She was able to handle so much more outside because she was dealing with so much less inside.

Refuturing Statements

♥ What if it's possible that it's safe
  for me to relax.

♥ What if it's possible that when I relax,
  I release what's been weighing me down
  and making me preoccupied and less effective.

♥ What if it's possible that when I relax,
  I can take in more of what I want and need.

♥ What if it's possible that releasing my S.T.U.F.F.
  is one of the most productive things I can do.

♥ What if it's possible that it's safe for me to be
  with my thoughts, my feelings, and myself.

105

Choose Statement

I choose to
breathe,
relax,
and receive.

Being Engaged

I was taking a class called Pole Basics early in my pole studies. In it, the teacher, Nikki, broke down common spins to help hone foundational moves.

We were doing a round-about into a pirouette, and Nikki came over to observe me. Her tip for me was not to relax into the round-about so much, but instead to stay in better control of my muscles to make the move more fluid.

One of my gifts is seeing connections and patterns in seemingly unrelated contexts. As I stood there after Nikki moved on, my mind started flying between the physical world of pole dancing and the energetic world of my work with clients and my overall understanding of life.

I work with lots of clients who have a stranglehold on life. Everything is about control—controlling their business, their relationships, and their lives. You name it, and they're controlling it. And it's *exhausting* for them.

In fact, I have yet to meet anyone who *hasn't* tried to control some aspect of life. I'm consistently watching to see where I'm micromanaging my life, instead of fully living it.

This desire for control comes from fear, and from experiences in the past when we felt like a victim with no control or influence over events in our lives. One of the big fears is that if we let go of control, everything will fall apart, and/or nothing will ever get done.

Part of my job is to help clients trust more and control less. We release the stuff from the past and the fears, and then move on to practices that help them expand their ability to trust themselves, other people, and the unfolding of Life.

The result is that they feel more and more in the flow of life. When they're able to relax, they have more fun in their relationships and their business, they're more productive, and everything unfolds with more ease and grace.

So how did Nikki's words that "more control will give more fluidity" fit in with this? Or did it?

As I did another round-about and focused on "control," I paid close attention to my body and what was happening there. Lean out, body strong yet fluid, shoulders down, core...

And it hit me.

What we were really talking about was ***engagement***. It was about keeping my muscles *engaged*. Not control in the sense of being rigid, which leads to injuries. Not relaxation in the sense of being saggy, which also leads to injuries. But engaged.

Take a minute now to do the following and see if you can feel the difference in your body.

Tighten your stomach muscles until they feel clenched. If you do it hard enough, your breathing becomes shallow and your shoulders curve over a bit.

With your muscles still clenched, try twisting your shoulders to look behind you. You don't get very far, do you?

Now let those same muscles completely go. Let your gut hang out. Your whole body slumps, and again you're taking shallow breaths, aren't you?

In this position, try again to twist your shoulders to look behind you. It's hard to move, isn't it?

Now, *engage* your stomach muscles while keeping your shoulders relaxed. Your body straightened and you're taking deeper breaths now, right?

What happens when you twist your body now?

When your muscles are toned and engaged—not rigid or slack—there is flow. Your circulation moves better, hormones levels are more stable, food is digested more thoroughly, and wastes are eliminated more easily.

There's also more flow in your energy. You have more stamina and more vitality. Your acupuncture meridians and your chakras are more vibrant. You're more alive.

This is true in how we approach life too.

When we're engaged in life, neither controlling or disconnected, we're more alive. We're more vibrant. We have more flow and more vitality. Sometimes we err on the side of pushing, trying to control Life, ourselves, and others. This makes us rigid and closed off. At other times we err on the side of looseness, not taking actions that are ours to take. We aren't showing up for Life, so very little happens.

When we show up, engaged with and open to what Life brings us, ready to do our part, magic happens.

Refuturing Statements

♥ What if it's possible for me to be both relaxed and engaged.

♥ What if it's possible that being relaxed and engaged gives me a greater capacity for flow.

♥ What if it's possible that when I'm relaxed and engaged, I'm more alert, creative, and productive.

♥ What if it's possible that when I'm relaxed and engaged, I feel more connected and have more fun.

Choose Statement

I choose to be relaxed and engaged as I take my next step.

How to Keep from Making Things Worse

Renee was a client of mine who was going through a challenging time. Her former business partner, Jean, had been unorganized, and client work wasn't getting done. So Renee bought her out and took over the business on her own.

On one of our calls, Renee was upset because Jean had begun bad-mouthing her and how she was running the business. This was happening on social media, both on Jean's personal page and on pages for communities in which both women participated.

The big problem was that a lot of the insults were insinuations, comments that were vague enough that Renee didn't feel like she could respond without making it a bigger deal than it already was.

The clients who had stayed through the transition were really happy, and many had told Renee how much better everything was running. Still, Renee was feeling pissed about Jean's snide comments.

She felt caught. If she ignored them, she worried that she

was being naïve, and that the situation might get really bad without her realizing it. What if Jean ruined her reputation and ran off her clients?

If she paid attention to them, she worried that she'd manifest *more* negativity and make the situation worse. She certainly didn't want to create a self-fulfilling prophecy and look for problems, yet she couldn't stop thinking about it.

She fluctuated between smiling and telling herself that it was all OK, and not to worry, and running through all the things she'd *really* like to say back to Jean.

And then there was the nagging worry about causation. Renee is a kind, very aware person who had done her best in her dealings with Jean for everything to be fair and above-board. She really didn't feel like she'd done anything to deserve this kind of treatment. Yet there was what she called her "LOA (Law of Attraction) voice" telling her that she had invited this situation in. She was beating herself up for having "created" this problem.

On top of all that, she knew it would be a good idea for her to keep connecting with her clients, but she was worried that she'd either drive them away with all the negativity she was feeling, or that one of them would ask her about something Jean said, and she'd lose it. If she didn't stay in touch, she was afraid that they'd feel neglected and leave.

All of this left her feeling super tense, and emotionally, physically, and energetically drained. No wonder she was exhausted!

I hear this dilemma from clients all the time. After

all, everyone knows that you create what you pay attention to. So what's the right thing to do?

First of all, the belief that there's a "right" and a "wrong" way to handle a situation adds pressure. It's easy to get stuck judging and blaming yourself, leaving you feeling tied up in knots. Let's start by changing our question.

What's an *effective* thing to do in a situation like this?

Remember that life is about your expansion and your greater expression of your essence. This isn't a test, and no one's out to get you. In Renee's case, it really looked like Jean was out to get her and ruin her business. Jean may even have thought that was what she was doing. The truth, though, is that Jean was acting out her own hurt and pain.

I haven't talked to Jean, so I don't know what her situation was. Maybe she regretted selling the company. Maybe she was having some financial problems and was hoping to get some clients away. Maybe her primary relationship was falling apart, and she was lashing out in anger. While I don't know what her motivation was, I do know that her behavior was *far* more about her than about Renee.

This is important for us all to keep in mind as we go about our lives. Yes, this is about not taking what happens in our lives personally. It's also about looking at our reactions. When we think we're reacting to something "out there," it's time to look inside at what we're worried about and what's unresolved in us.

Discovering what we haven't yet resolved is the gift we get when we approach challenging situations consciously. It's showing us what the next ring of S.T.U.F.F.. is that, when it's released, will give us access to more of our essence and more of our power.

Renee and I started the call with her telling me what was going on and just venting some. Not tons, but enough to let her mind relax. She then did some physical movement. Our bodies store our unresolved emotions, and Renee's body simply had to do some of its own releasing before she could move on.

Once her body and mind were calmer (not calm, but calmer), we could give space for her emotions to come up. I have clients touch specific acupressure points on their head and chest to facilitate the flow of energy. As Renee held those points, her energy began to move, and her emotions began to flow.

Renee wasn't "putting" any negativity into this situation. She wasn't focusing on the negative and creating what she didn't want. She was simply letting the tears, anger, hurt, and fear that were *already there* come up. Jean's words and actions were triggering Renee's old S.T.U.F.F. Our work was allowing it to naturally come up and be released.

The result was that Renee felt clearer, calmer, and more energized at the end of our call. She was able to see the whole situation with more clarity and far less emotion. Humorously and not surprisingly, she got a call from a client team shortly after we talked, and it went great. She told me that the team was eager for her help with a project, asked her lots of questions, and told her more than once how much smoother everything was since she'd taken over the business. And Renee was in a space to really hear and take that in.

The next time she heard something Jean said, Renee was able to think about it calmly and decide if there were actions she needed to take. She could clearly see the desperation behind Jean's actions. Renee's intuition told her that her best course of action was to continue reaching out to clients as part of her New Year's routine, letting them know she valued them, and seeing if there was anything they needed from her that they weren't getting. She realized she was showing up even more strongly on those calls and was having even more fun doing them after our call than before the situation with Jean came up.

Your emotions are the fuel that drives your manifestation. Ignoring your fears and worries doesn't help because they still have energy. Even if a big part of you wants more money, if you have a fear that being rich means you'll lose your friends and will end up alone, you'll have limited wealth at best.

Some people feel embarrassed or ashamed when they tell me some of their buried fears. They don't realize that it's an act of power, and that all I see is their courage and the new possibilities that are opening up for them. They don't know that I've worked with highly successful people who have very similar fears. They don't know that I've encountered the same thoughts and fears in myself.

I've worked with an international model, people who make over a million dollars a year, an international performer, an international speaker, several best-selling authors, and someone in the TV industry, among other successful business owners. I have clients fill out a form before each call describing what's going on for them, including the fears that are coming up. These are taken word-for-word from some of those pre-call forms:

- I just couldn't go out in front of people.

- I'm not good enough.

- I'm not good enough to charge for my services.

- I'm not worthy of receiving.

- It's hard for me to receive love, money.

- I'm afraid of my own power.

- I'm not good enough.

- I have a desire to collapse and hide.

- I'm overwhelmed.

- I'm afraid of not giving my clients what they need.

- I'm starting to shift bedrock beliefs, and I don't always want that.

- I hate what I do.

- My energy is going to turn people away.

- I'm so flawed for being this messed up.

- I'm afraid I'll be alone.

- I'm afraid of succeeding and not succeeding.

Recognize yourself in any of that?

When our S.T.U.F.F. gets triggered, it's a gift. The situation is shining a light on gunk that was buried in the dark, keeping us from being more fully ourselves. It's been clogging our connection with the Universe and with ourselves, and now that we're aware of it, we can do something about it.

Being triggered isn't permanent. You won't always feel this way. Here are notes from these same clients after our call.

- ♥ I feel light, much lighter.

- ♥ I feel grounded and peaceful.

- ♥ I feel bright and very calm. Anger that's always been there is gone. I feel joy.

- ♥ I'm at a whole new level since my sessions with you. You have helped me to step into my POWER! I am happier, calmer, and more confident.

- ♥ So many synchronicities are happening, and my team is working better than I dreamed we could.

- ♥ I feel like I'm seeing everyone differently. Worries that used to be there just aren't.

- ♥ Reconnecting with my family and being my full self feels wonderful!

- ♥ You helped me connect with and amplify

the light within. I now have the language to
stare down scary things and to find the courage
to love the scary things. I'm moving forward
with joy!

This is possible for you too.

Letting the S.T.U.F.F. come up can feel scary, embarrassing, painful, and/or really, really good. It gives you a
fresh, clear perspective so you can take inspired action.
You're not putting negativity out into the world, you're
clearing inner space for new possibilities and getting
access to more of your own power.

Situations like this call out a bigger version of you.
You get to experience yourself living more fully, uphold-
ing your commitments, and showing up in a bigger way.
If you're not sure what that looks like, play with it. Try
asking yourself, "What if it's possible that this is happening *for* me, not *to* me. What could this be opening up for
me? What is this an opportunity for?" By asking these
questions several times with lightness and curiosity, you
begin opening the way for new insights. You move out of
the victim role and into the role of the creator of your life.

Refuturing Statements

♥ What if it's possible for me to release old
thoughts and feelings that have kept me stuck.

♥ What if it's possible that doing this isn't putting
out negativity, but reconnecting me with my
own positivity and essence.

♥   What if it's possible that doing this connects me even more with my power and my purpose.

♥   What if it's possible that this situation is happening *for* me, not *to* me.

♥   What if it's possible for me to be more confident, creative, and connected with my power than I was before.

Choose Statement

I choose to be open to my feelings
and to new possibilities.

The Same Old Stories

No one can make you feel anything. You don't cause others' feelings, and they don't cause yours. So when you get pissed because someone cut you off in traffic, it's not about them, it's about you. It definitely might have startled or scared you, but the anger is *your* reaction.

When your child, significant other, or employee doesn't follow through on something important, a conversation needs to be had and a system may need to be created or adjusted. Feeling angry, betrayed, or powerless means something in your S.T.U.F.F. is getting triggered. Otherwise, it's simply a situation to be handled.

For years, I played an internal game to decide if my reaction to a situation was based on my S.T.U.F.F. being triggered or was the "fault" of the other person. When someone did something that left me feeling angry or powerless, I'd see if I could imagine even one person I knew who would have a different reaction. If I could, I would know that my reaction was about me, not about the situation.

For instance, when my husband got angry in traffic, and I felt myself withdrawing, I played the game. I could easily see one of my friends calling him on it and another responding with humor, so I knew that the withdrawal was about me. It wasn't inherent to the situation, and it certainly wasn't the only option.

This helped me own my actions and reactions. It also helped me see other possibilities for handling what was happening. And for the record, I never once had a situation where I couldn't think of someone who would handle it differently. That was really frustrating at times when it would have felt good to blame the other person for how I was feeling!

Repeating old patterns means that we're stuck in old stories. Withdrawing is something I did growing up whenever I felt scared or uncomfortable. It's still easy for me to go there if I don't stay alert for it. I can give you all kinds of reasons why I've done it and what other people did to "make me do it," but those are just my stories and justifications.

Retelling old stories is a way of keeping us in a victim role. It makes everything about the other person and what's happened in the past. It means we don't have to look at *ourselves* and our feelings. We don't have to be honest and vulnerable about our fears and our hurts. We also don't have to look at what we can do differently.

When a client shares a story with me of something that's happened to them in the past where a lot of their energy is stuck, I'm interested in the story to the extent that it helps them connect to their feelings.

Especially early in the process, people are very identified with what happened in the past. It feels real, tangible, and heavy. It can be important for them to talk about it, to have it witnessed, to look at it full on, and not hide from any of it or push any of it away.

It can be very cathartic for them to tell the story.

What I've seen over and over is that, the more those big experiences are released, the less and less of a need there is to talk about what happened. Sometimes clients will get part way through a story, then jump to realizations about what they've made it mean. The meaning is the S.T.U.F.F. I often make intuitive connections for them to other things that they've told me they've struggled with, so that the releasing goes even deeper.

As our work goes on, there's even less need to know what happened and what the emotion is connected with. Accessing and releasing the emotion is the gold, not discovering the details of the story.

There are times now when something gets triggered for me, and I'll have a big emotional release without knowing specifically what it's related to. That feels freeing, and like I'm dealing in the pure currency of emotion.

For example, I've been working a lot on this book and feeling super vulnerable about some of what I'm sharing. After dance the other night, I sat in my car and cried for 20 minutes. I have no idea why except that the movement and the writing released something that needed to come out through tears. The next day, I felt more at ease, and my writing started flowing even more.

Stories can be powerful. If you've had an experience that feels defining of who you are, I encourage you to explore that experience. Write the story. Tell it. Go into the details. Don't whitewash any of it. Don't dismiss any of your feelings. Allow yourself to really be with it and honor it.

What messages did you get from this experience?

What does it mean about you and for you?

Then get curious about it. Is there a different way to interpret it? Is there another possibility?

Looking back at your story, imagine that what the other person did was almost totally about them, about their fears, their insecurities, and their pain. How would that change your interpretation of what happened and what you've made it mean about you? If what happened wasn't about you being flawed or not good enough or wrong in some way, what *might* it have been about? Is there power here for you that you haven't yet claimed?

Here's an example.

I had a client who, when she was young, was told by her mother that she hugged too much. My client took this to mean that she needed too much, she loved too much, and she *was* too much.

She went back and looked at her story with this new sense of curiosity. I had her sit with possibilities like, "What if it's possible there was nothing wrong with me," and "What if it's possible my mother's reaction was about her and not about me."

What she saw was that she has a strong capacity to love and that her mother, for whatever reason, wasn't in a space at that time to receive it. When she looked back at the incident, she realized that she wasn't feeling needy. She was only wanting to express the big love she felt for her mom.

The message she got upon reflection was that not everyone is ready and willing to accept the love that she feels. She can both be her fiercely loving self and not overwhelm someone who doesn't seem ready to receive the full force of her love.

Try that now with your own story of something that's happened. You might want to start with a story that doesn't feel super heavy. Remember to go through this process with lightness, not trying to find an answer, but simply playing with the possibilities. This isn't about finding answers, but about your expansion and your willingness to be with what is and what was.

When we aren't honest about our feelings and aren't willing to look at our S.T.U.F.F., we stay stuck in our old stories. We're fighting against what's true for us. We're trying not to hurt. Often, we're trying to be the person we think we should be rather than the person we are, and that disconnects us from our power.

If we look at the stories we keep telling, we'll find the feelings and truths we've been denying. We'll do the courageous work of looking directly at our pain and seeing that it isn't who we are. It doesn't define us. The story isn't our truth. The things we've believed about ourselves isn't the truth. The story isn't who we are.

Our essence is our truth, and our essence is love.

Refuturing Statements

♥ What if it's possible that what happened was not my fault.

125

♥   What if it's possible that there's
       another way to see this.

♥   What if it's possible that my old point of view
       was OK, that it's what made sense to me,
       and that it's the best I knew at the time.

♥   What if it's possible for me to entertain
       new possibilities and new ways
       of interpreting what happened.

♥   What if it's possible for me to release
       where I've been stuck in this old story,
       this old situation, and to integrate it into
       my understanding of myself from a place
       of curiosity, love, and compassion.

♥   What if it's possible that there are more
       possibilities here than I ever realized.

Choose Statement

I choose to view my past
with compassion, honesty,
curiosity, and possibility.

Your Weakness
Is Your Superpower

Most of us think that there's something about us that doesn't really "work," that could be better. Most of us have tried self-improvement in some form or another. We're sure that if we were better, life would work better for us. We'd have more flow. Abundance would come more easily. We'd be more accepted, more confident...better.

It's painful when we try to mold ourselves to fit in, to be like everyone else. And yet it's a constant thing for so many people.

Even non-conforming can be a way of fitting in. If you're "fighting the status quo" the same way all your friends are, you might be conforming with *them*.

If you're judging those who look, think, dress, or live in a way that seems weird to you, you're part of the conforming movement. And remember, if we're harsh and judgmental with others, we're doing it to ourselves, too. We just may be more subtle about it.

For me, I've always wanted to "fix" that:

- Making a decision can be agonizing for me. I'm

not the one to ask where to eat or what movie to watch.

- I'm interested in and passionate about things that most people find weird. Those things have become more mainstream now, but energy work, enlightenment, and consciousness exploration were definitely "fringe" when I started, and I often felt on the outside.

- I'm acutely aware of energy, both inside me and in my surroundings, and haven't known what to do with it. I've felt at times that I can't hold it all in my body without exploding.

- I had so much love to express that I felt "over the top" with it. I thought this made me weak and "too much," and I worked to hold it in.

- I see the glass half full, with more on the way. I felt like this meant I was frivolous, uncool, and a lightweight.

A couple of years ago, I went to a workshop on identifying your genius, that thing that makes you special. As part of the registration process, the leader, Karen, asked for our birth information. Part of the workshop involved reading our charts for a system called Human Design that combines astrology, chakras, I Ching, and Kabbalah.

It's OK if that makes you want to roll your eyes. Keep reading, because that's not the important part.

When I got to the workshop, the first thing Karen said to me was, "Is your birth time right, because if so, that's weird?" I had no idea *why* it was weird, but I wasn't surprised. I'd always felt like I was weird.

Looking around at other people's charts, I could see mine was different. Theirs had a lot more color. Mine looked like the printer had run out of ink.

During the workshop, Karen told me that, according to Human Design, I'm in an aura group called Reflector that's 1 percent of the population. To put it in perspective, there are only four aura groups: 70 percent are Generators, 20 percent are Projectors, and 9 percent are Manifestors. I'm the outlier. In fact, I was the first Reflector she'd ever had in a workshop.

Some of the characteristics of Reflectors include having a really hard time making decisions, not having a clearly defined sense of self, and being acutely sensitive to energy. When Reflectors are living in alignment with their design, they experience delight. They're more connected to the greater design for life than the "real world." These were all the things that I'd seen as being "bad" or "wrong" with me my whole life!

The kicker was seeing that my chart in particular, in two very prominent positions, says that I'm "a natural conduit and medium for love's expression here on Earth."

I cried tears of relief during the workshop.

I felt seen in a deep way that I didn't know I'd been missing, and I understood myself in a way I never had before. I began to accept the things about myself that I'd always tried to change, get rid of, or hide. Even better, by understanding my weirdness, I began to understand the gifts of it.

129

I have a hard time making decisions because I see so many perspectives and understand many points of view. Not having a clearly defined sense of self and being acutely sensitive to energy help me to be deeply connected to the Universe and to what's wanting to be recognized in others. I can hold space for clients in a way that's truly centered on them.

And my focus on love? Well, now that I'm more centered in myself and appreciating my own value, I'm able to use my powerful love to help clients blast through their blocks to receiving love. It clears out what needs to go and holds space for what's ready to emerge.

These are the gifts I bring to my clients. What I'd once tried to change or deny about myself is exactly what makes me so good at what I do!

In the workshop, Karen said over and over that our gifts are a problem until we realize that they're our gifts— and it's true! Accepting your weirdness is great and necessary. *Claiming* your weirdness as a strength, and learning to use it consciously and responsibly, makes you far more valuable to the people in your life. Until then, it feels like a weakness and a handicap. A problem.

This reminds me of one of my clients whose parents and teachers would get frustrated with how many questions she asked and the way she wanted to dissect ideas and things everyone took for granted. Those are the exact qualities that make her a creative genius and an innovative teacher.

Another client has a penetrating way of seeing into others that made people around her uncomfortable, even angry, as she was growing up. Now, she masterfully uses her gift as a coach, and her clients are grateful.

So instead of trying to follow the footsteps of others, spend some time discovering your weirdness—aka your gift. There may be a lot of old stuff to let go of around it because it's also felt like a failing and a weakness. You may even have been criticized, teased, or shamed for it.

Do whatever helps you get to know yourself better. Take personality inventories like the MBTI (Myers-Briggs Type Indicator), determine your Enneagram type, take a workstyles inventory. Just remember that you are all of that *and more*. Let those things help you get to know yourself, and then don't be limited by the results.

Keep looking inside. Notice how you feel in different situations and with different people. Keep experimenting to see what feels energizing and light, what brings you joy.

Become an expert on *you*. See what calls to your soul in each moment and honor it.

Refuturing Statements

- ♥ What if it's possible that I'm OK, just as I am.

- ♥ What if it's possible that I have strengths and gifts that I haven't recognized yet.

- ♥ What if it's possible that even the things I haven't liked about myself might be OK and acceptable.

- ♥ What if it's possible that even the things I haven't liked about myself could be part of my strengths and gifts.

♥ What if it's possible for me to have
a new understanding about the things
I haven't liked about myself.

♥ What if it's possible for me to be pleasantly
surprised by what I discover about myself.

Choose Statement

I choose to be open to the possibility
that I have more strengths and
gifts than I can imagine.

Curls

This may sound shallow to you, but I felt like my "differentness" was embodied in my hair.

My sisters have beautiful, silky hair. Theirs is that perfect blend of straight with body. You could call it gently waving.

My hair is curly. Really curly.

Over the years, I've gone through periods of sleeping with it in pin curls, spending 30 minutes or more a day with hot rollers, having it chemically straightened (sort of a reverse perm), keeping it pulled back…anything and everything I could think of to "make it behave."

I've cried more than once about my hair, feeling like it never looked good and certainly never cooperated with any of the popular styles. And I wasn't alone. I was once on a call with a group of five women who all happened to have curly hair. I mentioned that I felt like I needed to do an energy release around having grown up with curly hair, and every one of them got excited about the idea and wanted in.

If this sounds over the top to you, just substitute whatever it is about yourself that you've felt embarrassed about. My hair was one of my things, but as far as I've seen, we *all* have had at least one "thing."

Especially as a teenager and young adult, I so wanted to fit in. I wanted to be spectacularly normal.

Years have passed, the internet has happened, books have been published, and I now know how to take care of my curls. I know how to nourish them, how to style them, and how to have them cut. I've grown in my confidence and am OK with my hair taking up space and being so visible.

The result is that I now *love* my curls!

They are *perfect* for me! They're playful and quirky and sensual, and they seriously don't behave some days. It seems like when I get too serious, they stick out and do odd things. When I honor them and take care of them, they shine. They are gorgeous. I wouldn't be me without my curls.

It all changed when I surrendered. When I accepted the fact that I have curly hair and stopped trying to make it be something it wasn't. There are some styles that I'll never wear. I'll never be the woman in the convertible with her hair blowing behind her. I'll be the one whose hair dances and does what it wants. My curls have a mind of their own. They're raucous. They're untamable. They are freedom.

Body shame and embarrassment aren't just women's issues. Every man I've talked to has dealt at times with some feeling of physical inferiority. Even people I know who have stellar bodies have wrestled with something.

This is a problem because being ashamed of or disconnected from our bodies diminishes our power. *Every-*

one gets power from being in their bodies, and you can't be fully in your body and hating it at the same time.

When we're ashamed of our bodies—whether it's because of our teeth, our complexion, our shape, our hair, or anything else—we can't show up fully. We can't let ourselves be fully seen.

If having braces or surgery or wearing a wig or working out helps you feel more confident in your body, go for it. And if it doesn't, that's fine too. Do what allows you to show up more in your power and your grandness.

Just make sure you aren't trying to be perfect. Don't wait until you're "done" to show up. The opposite of perfect is authentic, so start with showing up where you are right now.

There are times when I go to pole class and hear the woman next to me calling herself old, and she's nine years younger than I am. Or I'm taking turns on a pole with a woman who's 20 years younger than I am and was a college athlete. I find myself wishing I'd walked more, done more Pilates and less sitting over the years. And this is where I am. It's only by embracing where I am now and loving my body as it is that I can work *with* it. Pushing myself beyond my healthy limits serves no one.

The same is true of my energy. Pushing myself to work past my point of genuine productivity doesn't serve. Pushing myself to do things for my business that don't feel aligned for me doesn't serve.

What serves is staying engaged. What serves is doing what brings me joy. What serves is letting myself be seen.

It can be hard to find the balance. How do you know

when you're pushing in a positive or negative way? After all, just sitting there won't get you the fuller life you want. Sometimes I have to push myself to stay in a dance class. To make one more attempt at climbing the pole, to do one more pullup, to hold a plank just a little longer.

The difference is staying engaged with my bigger vision, with the *reason* I'm doing the challenging thing, and accepting that sometimes I'll err on one side or the other.

I have a client named Gigi who was pushing herself to market her new workshop. She *hated* writing the copy and sending out announcements. Every step felt draining, like she was having to manufacture the fuel to keep herself going. She couldn't understand the problem. She'd run this workshop several times before fairly successfully.

I helped her connect with her body to see what was going on. She felt a heaviness in her stomach and on her shoulders. In connecting with her heart, she realized that, while she loves teaching and likes the workshop topic well enough, it wasn't in alignment with what her heart was calling her to do.

What emerged was a strong inner pull to step into something new, to do more mentoring. and to work at a deeper level with clients. Checking in again with her body, the heaviness was gone, and her heart felt excited. I helped her connect with her heart through some inner conversations, which connected her to her creativity in a deeper way. I could see the difference immediately in the way her face became radiant and her eyes sparkled. Her smile was magnetic.

Writing copy for this new mentoring group was challenging. Gigi had to move through the fears that it brought up for her. Things like, was she ready for this step, would anyone sign up, and did she really have anything meaningful to teach people. She had to put her bum in the chair and actually do the work of writing.

Now, though, she was moving *toward* this new vision and was excited about it. She had the fuel she needed and got a refill each time she sat and connected with her vision and thought of the people she could serve, which I encouraged her to do every day.

It wasn't marketing she hated, as she had thought. It was marketing something that wasn't in alignment with her that really sucked.

Over the next weeks, I supported her in expanding into this new vision for herself and her business. It was a big catalyst for her. She released a lot of old S.T.U.F.F., created tons of inner space, and embraced more of who she is. Having done that initial workshop several times, she was ready for more. This course correction toward a greater leadership role meant that she was now *embodying* more of her essence. Scary? Yes. Energizing? Definitely, as the light in her eyes clearly showed.

Refuturing Statements

- ♥ What if it's possible there's something that's calling to me as my next step.

- ♥ What if it's possible that it doesn't matter if it's something new or improving something I've been doing.

♥ What if it's possible that what matters
is how it resonates with and energizes me.

♥ What if it's possible for me to know
what this is.

♥ What if it's possible for me to know what
it is and to take action toward creating it.

♥ What if it's possible that I am ready for this.

♥ What if it's possible that I can do this.

Choose Statement

I choose to honor what works
for me and to take my next step.

Measuring the Universe's Love

I recently worked with a client, Mattie, who identified her biggest issue as stress over her ability to generate income. She felt like she was "grabbing, grasping, and desperate." I've heard similar things from lots of clients.

When we use money to measure our success, it's just like in the board game Monopoly: we're either "winning" or "losing." And winning, in Monopoly as well as in most cultures, means amassing the most money, with the richest people being given special status and privileges. Seen through this lens, it's easy to see why most people concentrate their manifestation work on improving their finances.

But doing so has some unintended outcomes. For one thing, there will always be someone who's richer than you are, so being money-centric constantly calls your sense of self-worth into question. Having less money means you're less worthy. There's something you're not doing right. Life isn't smiling on you. You're not a "good manifestor."

Ironically, these very thoughts lower your vibration and make it harder for you to receive what you want. Feeling unworthy and "less than" also makes it harder for you to show up as your full self and take your next steps. It leaves you questioning whether the Universe really does love you, because it sure doesn't look or feel like it! This energy drain can quickly spiral downward.

Being money-centered also means that your attention is on what you can *get*. It's part of the "power over" dynamic where you're trying to feel safe and OK by bringing things in from the outside. This gives the Safety Self a megaphone to shout its fears and worries because you're dependent on the scary outer world. You're left trying to control what's outside of you, and you just can't do it.

Manifesting more money can feel like a big win, but often, as people reach their financial goals, they realize that they still don't feel safe or satisfied. The accumulation of money doesn't create connection or a sense of peace. Money appeals to the mind. It doesn't speak to the heart or the soul.

Shifting away from money as the measure of success changes the whole paradigm.

The first step in making this shift is to get, on more and more levels, that you're already safe and OK. Simply by virtue of the fact that you're here, you're worthy of love, connection, and abundance. You have gifts and a light to shine. You are loved by the Universe.

Your relationship with the Universe is not unlike your relationship with a romantic partner. When you know in every part of you that the person you're with loves you, you understand that flowers, dinner, compliments, and check-ins are all expressions of that love. Even when you have a disagreement, you trust the love hasn't evaporated. You know that things are moving in a positive direction, even if they look and feel messy in the moment.

The more fully you get that the Universe fucking loves you, the more you can be present with whatever's going on in your life. You trust that you're OK and are moving in a positive direction, even when it looks messy in the moment. You have a consistent undercurrent of knowing you're safe and cared for. This frees you to try new things, to be more yourself, and to worry less and enjoy more.

This leads to the second step of centering your energy in yourself.

When your energy is centered in yourself rather than outside of you, you're more grounded. You're also connected with your inner wisdom and your truth. This then becomes the place from which you make decisions, act, and share. You're presenting a more genuine version of yourself to the world.

This is fulfilling because the more you show up as who you truly are, the more seen and loved you are. It sounds so easy, and yet it can be the toughest thing to do!

A Real-World Example

I'm rewriting this chapter at a suggestion from my editor, and it's taken me longer to rewrite this one thing than I spent writing the entire rest of the book! There are several reasons why that's true. I definitely find it easier to write when I'm off by myself and when I have spacious time to meditate and be in nature. Another big factor, though, is that I've been sharing about the book a bit on Facebook and with a few people, and people are so excited about it! Christine's just agreed to write to the foreword, too. Suddenly, I'm feeling the pressure to have the book be *good*.

Before, when I was holed up writing, I was deep in my own process. I was connected with myself and what was wanting to be written. I was focused on simply sharing myself. Once I started getting excitement from other people, it brought up my fears of not living up to expectations, and wanting to please them.

I'm sharing this with you because it's a perfect illustration of the importance of our focus. When we focus on an outside result we're aiming for—whether it's getting money or pleasing someone—we start losing connection with ourselves. When we start on the inside—getting centered and being connected with our truth and what's emerging in us to be shared—we get back into our flow. Children naturally come from this space when they're given a safe, supportive environment. It's our nature.

The more you let the crap come up without judgment, reveal your authentic self, and share *from there*, the more abundant you'll be in all respects. Not only will money flow more easily, but so will your creativity, ingenuity, and strength. Your connections will be deeper and more meaningful because the people who like you are seeing and liking you for *you*, not a projection of who you think you need to be in order to earn more money. You're more fulfilled on every level.

By shifting your focus away from outer results and

toward showing up and sharing who you are, you let go of a dependence on what happens "out there" to make you feel safe and happy. This leads to greater self-expression and to you sharing the light that you came here to be.

When we pursue money as the goal, we get so caught up in what we "should" do and what's worked for others, that we don't live the life that makes us happy. We follow the recommendations of the Safety Self and other people out of a sense of desperation and need. But there's no amount of padding that will protect you from the waves of life. It's far more effective to let the waves wash over you and to dance with them.

Martin came to me struggling to make a decision. He was getting advice and pressure from several sources, each telling him to do something different. There was pressure not to waste money, not to waste time, and not to risk "getting in trouble" or making someone else upset.

I helped him let go of all of that noise and tune into his body and his inner guidance. As I stated each of his options, he was able to feel in his body and his emotions what was resonant for him. He was no longer trying to make his decision out of fear or compliance, but from his deeper wisdom and creativity. Even though the step he was guided to take felt scary, it also felt liberating and empowering.

When he followed through and took action, Martin felt expansive and free. That's a sign that you're in alignment with your essence and your truth. Playing small and denying who you are just to fit in will never give you that feeling, no matter how many "shoulds" and rules you're following.

The Universe loves you so fucking much that it wants freedom, joy, and love for you. This doesn't mean you should ignore money. Disregarding money as not being "spiritual" can be a way of hiding from discomfort around both having and not having it. I don't advocate hiding from *anything*.

Besides, the need for money can be a great motivator to have us do the important work of sharing our gifts. It can keep us from getting too complacent or too stuck, and is a fabulous way for us to uncover our S.T.U.F.F. around worthiness and receiving.

However, when we think that it's just us, little ole us, against the great big world, *of course* we look for something or someone outside of us to make us feel safe. Of course we feel that we need money, an assured position in a company, an assured role as a partner—a rescuer in some form or another. Nothing outside of us will ever fill us. It's like eating only white rice. It doesn't have the nutrients you need, so your body isn't getting what it needs, and you keep eating more. No matter how much you eat, you'll never be satisfied.

Maturing in who we are means becoming more and more connected to ourselves rather than looking to people and things to complete us. We fill ourselves from the inside, so we come to the world ready to share rather than needing to be filled. We don't *need* the job, the relationship, or accolades in order to feel abundant, safe, and worthy. Now we can relax and enjoy what Life brings us.

When we *know* that we are fucking loved by the Universe, are worthy of that love, can accept that love, and trust in that love, there is no outer situation that we can't weather. No amount of money is too little or too much for us to handle. Nothing anyone else says or does can make us not OK. We may feel sad, lonely, scared, or whatever else as we live this human experience, and we're still okay.

Focusing on sharing yourself, rather than on what you can get, puts you in prime manifesting energy. Not only that, but you're also in prime receiving energy because you're not grasping, comparing, or feeling unworthy. Life is given the chance to show up, and will often bring things that you didn't even know you wanted.

Refuturing Statements

- ♥ What if it's possible that the Universe really does fucking love me.

- ♥ What if it's possible that this is always true, including when it doesn't feel true.

- ♥ What if it's possible for me to see and feel the Universe's love for me.

- ♥ What if it's possible for me to trust in that love even when I don't see or feel it.

- ♥ What if it's possible that I am lovable, loved, and worthy of abundance.

- ♥ What if it's possible that it's OK for me to shine.

- ♥ What if it's possible for me to show up in the way that's right for me.

145

Choose Statement

I choose to focus on my
expression, expansion, service,
and sharing my gifts.

There's Gold
in the Shit

Cassie was one of my early clients. She got on the phone with me once and said, "Can I be honest with you?" I laughed and said, "Please!"

She hesitated. "I don't always look forward to our calls."

I encouraged her to tell me more.

"Working with you, I have to look at stuff I don't want to look at. Sometimes it feels really intense and uncomfortable. I've worked really hard to be successful, in part so I didn't have to deal with this stuff! I figured if I made enough money, I wouldn't feel money pressure anymore, and I'd be more confident. I don't like to feel the stuff that I do when I work with you."

As she spoke, I could feel Cassie's panic at not feeling in control. I heard her unspoken words that she was struggling with something big. Reassuring her would calm her Safety Self and let her decide if she was ready to move forward.

"Cassie," I said. "You know you can stop at any time.

You're in control here. I know that you're an amazing woman. If you said you wanted to stop, I wouldn't think any less of you."

She took a deep breath.

"I know, but I don't want to stop. My way wasn't working. I mean, I *am* successful, but it's such a struggle, and I know I could be *more* successful if I could get out of my own way. But I still don't like this."

"You don't like feeling all of this."

"No! I don't! It feels scary and painful."

"Why do you keep coming back?"

"Because I feel better after."

All her life, Cassie had been doing what so many of us do—controlling her feelings to keep things from getting too bad.

Imagine your emotions traveling in a wave pattern. Sometimes you're going up the wave, sometimes you're coming down. What most people do, once they sense themselves going down, is to start madly kicking to bring themselves up again. They fight the downward motion.

What they don't know is that there's something at the bottom of the waves that needs to be felt and acknowledged. Not going there simply delays connecting with it. It doesn't make the feeling go away. And it takes a *lot* of energy. Like Cassie said, it creates a *lot* of struggle.

The great thing about going to the bottom of the wave is that you'll naturally bob back up as soon as you've fully felt whatever was there.

Sounds easy, right?

Well, as Cassie said, it's *not* always easy. Especially

if you've spent 30, 40, 50 years or more avoiding the bottom of the wave. That's a lot of stuff to feel and a very engrained pattern to shift.

Thinking Your Feelings

It's also hard because most people haven't been taught how to *feel* their feelings. Does that sound crazy? It did to another client, Teri. Teri had always thought of herself as being very emotional. She cried pretty easily, got angry pretty often, and could swing from one to the other.

What she'd never realized is that when she was angry, she'd think angry thoughts. She'd tell someone about what was making her angry. She would yell and express her rage and frustration, sometimes to the person she was mad at, sometimes to other people.

When Teri was sad, she'd cry. In her mind, she'd play through what was happening and why the situation was so bad. She'd have thoughts like, "This isn't fair. This isn't what I signed up for. This isn't how it's supposed to go. I hate this." And she'd cry. She'd even enroll other people into seeing how bad it was and how wrong the other person had been to make her feel this way.

The thing is that emotions are body-centered, and Teri was almost exclusively in her head. She wasn't feeling the pain, the deep sadness, the rage. Truly *feeling* these goes beyond words. You get to a point when you're fully in your body, feeling. Words drop away, and you just *feel*.

Teri didn't realize how much she was using her stories of loss and abuse to feel connected to other people. Part

149

of her needed to stay at the bottom of the wave because that's when people rallied around her. Her Safety Self was afraid that if people didn't feel sorry for her, they'd leave. She could be sad and connected, or happy and alone.

Of course, Teri didn't realize this. She wasn't consciously manipulating people or intentionally staying stuck in her story. She honestly didn't feel like people really *got* how awful things had been for her. In a sense, that's true. No one else had lived her experiences. No one else had the deep knowing that she had of just how painful it all had been.

The thing is, though, that Teri was the one who needed to feel all of that. Like my experience at the retreat when I wailed my pain at my daughter's death. No one in that room could feel that except me.

Where Cassie was kicking to stay off the ocean floor, Teri was scooting sideways, staying on the bottom, but not at the spot where she would really feel her pain. Even though their methods were different, they were both avoiding the feeling.

We keep ourselves from going here because it hurts. It can be to a lesser or greater degree depending on what we're grieving and how much S.T.U.F.F. is attached to it. But not feeling it doesn't make it go away. It just doesn't.

There's a reason, though, that Cassie and Teri kept working with me. Cassie said it well:

"I feel so much better after our calls. It's like I'm getting parts of me back, and like I'm learning how to be a friend to myself instead of my own worst enemy. I'm more relaxed—not totally relaxed, but I'm getting there.

150

And life's starting to feel easier. I'm doing things I used to put off, and it doesn't feel like a big deal."

What Cassie's pointing to is the way she's reclaiming her power.

The more she feels her feelings and addresses these areas she's been avoiding, the more power she gets back. It's like the way that some societies used the threat of curses to keep possible robbers away from tombs. The more treasure was hidden, the bigger the curses. In fact, the size of the curses indicated the size of the treasure.

It's the same with your feelings. Those things you most dread addressing are the very areas where most of your power is stored. You can always start small and take care of some of the less intense stuff first. This helps build up your confidence and your energy, and it gives you evidence that what you're doing works. When you're ready (and when you have help if you want it), you can move on to some of the bigger things.

Refuturing Statements

♥ What if it's possible that it's safe for me to feel my feelings.

♥ What if it's possible that feeling uncomfortable or scared doesn't mean that I'll always feel that way.

♥ What if it's possible that it's safe for me to go to the bottom of the wave, and safe for me to come up again.

♥   What if it's possible that all I need to do
        is to breathe and allow my feelings to flow.

♥   What if it's possible that I can do this
        in the time and way that's right for me.

♥   What if it's possible that help
        is available for me.

Choose Statement

I choose to embrace
new possibilities
as I take each step.

Why We Don't Do
What We Know to Do

You may have read suggestions in this book and thought, "I know to do that! Why don't I just do what I know to do?"

My client Monica knows that frustration. On one of our early calls, she was wrestling with frustration and low energy. I asked her to keep a gratitude journal every day between then and our next call. "OK, here's a question for you," she said. "I've known for years that I should do that. Why haven't I?"

I had her put one hand on top of the other over the center of her chest (over her heart chakra) and ask herself that question. I recommended that she ask with a sense of gentle curiosity—not looking for an answer, but simply exploring the question to see what came up.

Several things surfaced:

■ It felt like trouble and extra effort.

■ When she was feeling good, it didn't feel like she needed to go to the trouble. When she felt down, she didn't have the energy to do it, so it just never got done.

- There was a tightness in her chest when she thought about it. As she sat noticing the tightness, this thought surfaced: "If I say I'm grateful for my husband, it means I have to stay with him, and I'm feeling really ambivalent about my marriage, but I feel guilty if I don't say I'm grateful for him."

Whether the thing you're not doing is a gratitude journal, exercise, or something else, Monica's findings point the way to why you're probably not doing it.

It Takes Effort

As comedian John Mulaney says, it's 100 percent easier NOT to do something. Life is busy already. There has to be a reason for us to put in the effort to do something on top of what we're already doing. Otherwise, we'll opt for the easier route of doing nothing. The key here is to be connected with your commitment. Why do you want to do this thing (or think it's a good idea to do it)?

Common reasons include:

- It'll make me healthier / happier / wealthier.

- I'll feel better.

- It'll get me a step closer to this bigger thing I want to be, do, or have.

- I love the person who'll benefit from this, and it'll really make a difference for them.

- Giving my time, energy, or abundance to someone else increases my feeling of love and makes me feel connected to my community.

A word of caution: If your reason is something that feels heavy or carries resentment, like, "It'll get my boss off my back," then keep looking. Find a why statement that brings you a sense of lightness and joy, or it'll still feel like you're dragging a boulder behind you.

Not Using Habit

Habits and routines are powerful things. I imagine you can think of at least one thing you do regularly that you would consider to be a bad habit. It can be challenging to start something new, but if you use the power of habit for good, it can make a tremendous difference.

I've heard repeatedly that anything you do for 21 days becomes a habit. I don't know if I'm particularly hard to train (my dog and cat seem to have managed it), but 21 doesn't seem to be the magic number for me. On someone else's recommendation, I set up an 8-week chart to track 3 habits I wanted to add to my day: meditation, movement, and energy exercises. I added some color and a nice border to the chart so that I felt drawn to it. I also set up some accountability for myself in a Facebook group. That worked much better for me.

One of my clients created a chart that incorporated several elements. Not only did it have the days for her to check off, but across the top she put her goal and, beneath it, a supporting Choose Statement. On the left-hand side of the page, she put an image and quote that were inspiring for her.

I encourage you to get creative. The more lightness, beauty, and fun you bring to this process, the more likely you are to keep at it. Remember to keep your eyes on the prize.

There's a Deeper Issue

Monica's last insight about her ambivalence and guilt was a big hurdle for this particular practice. If you can't seem to get yourself to do something, you may well have S.T.U.F.F. that's getting in the way.

For Monica, it was the thought that if she was grateful for something, she'd be "stuck" with it, like it was. She didn't know that by feeling grateful for what we have, as it is, we actually create space for it to evolve or for something even better to come in.

To find out what's holding you back, you need to connect more deeply with yourself. You can do this through journaling, talking it out with someone, noticing what's going on in your body and getting curious about it, paying attention to your dreams ... however you get insights.

If you're still having trouble unearthing the block, try playing with the prompt, "If I were to do this habit regularly, then ..." See how many different endings you can come up with. Initially, they're likely to sound positive. After a bit, you'll start getting down to the block.

What Does Your Heart Want?

The phrase, "My heart isn't in it," evolved for a very good reason. If you're trying to make yourself do something that your inner wisdom doesn't support, it's going to be an uphill climb.

The way to check it is to notice how you *feel*—physically and emotionally—when you think of doing the practice. Does it excite you and feel light, or does it feel heavy? What "should" thoughts do you have around it? You may be excited about getting healthier, but the *type* of exercise you have in mind doesn't sound fun. Instead of running, your body and soul might want to dance. Instead of a sitting meditation, your soul might want to do tai chi.

Try approaching the question of the habit with a sense of lightness. Ask yourself, "If I could do anything to help me meet my goal, what would I do? What would be fun and help me feel more energized?"

You Might Need Support

Many of us have gotten the idea somehow that strength means we don't need help from anyone. Pure BS. If you can create your dream life without help, your dream isn't very big, and it isn't stretching you very much. That's fine if that's the conscious choice you want to make.

If, however, you want a big life, you need help along the way.

I wouldn't be where I am today without the teachers, mentors, coaches, friends, and family that I've had. Not anywhere *close* to here.

It's taken time, energy, money, and huge commitment for me to keep engaging with the people who've supported me, and it's been worth every bit of it.

My standard is to always choose a person, program, or project that scares me in the right way. The right way means that my Safety Self is nervous—sometimes *really* nervous. Whether it's about the money, the time away from my family, the bigness of the project (like writing a book!), or something else, for something to be worth my time and energy, it needs to expand me.

This doesn't mean that my life is drudgery. On the contrary. My life is more fun now than ever, and it keeps getting better. The more I stretch, the easier it gets and the more I find others who want to stretch and play with me. I also get less and less attached to the fear. It feels more like the adrenaline of a rollercoaster ride.

When I got serious about writing this book, I hired an editor/coach. When I wanted to take quantum steps in my leadership, I signed on for a 10-month intensive program. I hire coaches and participate in mentoring groups. I have frequent conversations with people who help me stay aware, and I regularly listen to a recording or read a book from someone who inspires me. The more supported I am, the bigger my life becomes.

Remember That It's a Process

You spent many years doing things the old way. That's a deeply ingrained pattern. Changing it can be like trying to turn an ocean liner, requiring time and space. Thankfully, changing it won't take the same number of years that you spent building the old habit, and the more you let go of your S.T.U.F.F., the more quickly it'll happen.

When you don't do what you know to do, it's simply a missed opportunity to take a step in owning your power. There will be others. The big thing is not to turn to it into a downward spiral. Beating yourself up for not having done what you intended to do only makes it worse.

Imagine a toddler falling and saying to herself, "I can't believe I fell again. How stupid of me! I'll bet other kids are walking already. I took two steps yesterday. I thought I'd be up to at least five today! How am I ever going to learn to run if I can't even walk to the sofa? I'll never get the hang of this!"

Maybe there's a reason our biggest spurts of development happen before our reasoning brain comes online. Just remember that thinking something doesn't mean it's true, so you don't need to believe your thoughts.

A powerful way of handling a missed opportunity is the 3 Cs—curious, creative and courageous.

Get curious. Notice how it feels in your body. What are your emotions? What are your thoughts? How important was this to you? What were you prioritizing higher than your goal? In other words, what made you say yes to whatever you did instead of the beneficial thing you wish you had done?

Get creative. Are there systems like a chart or accountability that you want to set up? Are there reminders that would be helpful? Is there something you want to do to take care of the S.T.U.F.F. that's blocking you? Is there a way to make it more fun and appealing? Is there someone you want to support you or guide you?

Get courageous. There are all kinds of things you can do to make taking your next step easier. The more S.T.U.F.F. you let go of, the easier it'll be. Tools like Amy Cuddy's Power Posing and Mel Robbins' 5-Second Rule can be really helpful. You can listen to the recording of the Refuturing Statements that you've downloaded from my website, or get your energy moving by dancing to your favorite song.

At the end of the day, though, you still have to take the step. You. It may feel like walking through fire, but I *guarantee* it'll be worth it. Every hard step you take— every single one—connects you more with your power. When you know that and breathe it in, the connection is even stronger.

Remember to Celebrate

When you do make a step, even a very small one, celebrating it will build your momentum. It helps you focus on what's going well and on your progress, rather than focusing on what you haven't done.

It also helps you own the power you've reclaimed with that step. Otherwise, it's like planting and tending a field, then never harvesting and eating your crops. Taking the time to integrate the energy from what you did can be a great thing to do at the end of your day. If your Safety Self pops in with something you haven't done yet, write it down if you need to. Otherwise, just say, "Thanks. I'm focusing now on what I *did* get done." It'll get easier and easier.

I leave you with these last Refuturing Statements, and lots and lots of love. You've got this. You are divine. The Universe fucking loves you, just as you are. From here, it's just a game of expansion and exploration.

Refuturing Statements

♥ What if it's possible that I can do this.

♥ What if it's possible I'm ready, more ready than I realize or would dream is possible.

♥ What if it's possible that everything in my life has prepared me for this moment and this step.

♥ What if it's possible that I am more loved, more supported, and more capable than I ever imagined possible.

♥ What if it's possible that, even if this doesn't turn out like I plan, that that's OK, and I can handle it.

♥ What if it's possible it can turn out even bigger and better than I hope it will.

♥ What if it's possible that all I have to do is breathe and take my next step.

♥ What if it's possible that I can do this and that I'm ready.

♥ What if it's possible that this is possible for me.

♥ What if it's possible that the Universe fucking loves me and is always conspiring for my highest good and greatest joy.

Choose Statement

I choose to accept the love,
support, and opportunities
that feel resonant for me.
I choose to take my next step.

Resources

It's important to feed yourself well—body, mind, and spirit. Whatever you take in affects your energy, including the conversations you have, the movies you watch, the books you read, and the music you listen to.

Nurturing yourself with positivity keeps your energy up and your vibration high.

Here's a list of books that I've enjoyed, covering a wide range of topics.

The Four Agreements
 by don Miguel Ruiz and Peter Coyote

Love Warrior: A Memoir
 by Glennon Doyle

Rejection Proof: How I Beat Fear and Became Invincible Through 100 Days of Rejection
 by Jia Jiang

Year of Yes: How to Dance It Out, Stand in the Sun and Be Your Own Person
 by Shonda Rhimes

Braving the Wilderness: The Quest for True Belonging and the Courage to Stand Alone
 by Brené Brown

*How to Be Here: A Guide to Creating
a Life Worth Living,*
>by Rob Bell

*The Soul of Money: Reclaiming the Wealth
of Our Inner Resources*
>by Lynne Twist

*The 5 Second Rule: Transform your Life, Work,
and Confidence with Everyday Courage*
>by Mel Robbins

*The Book of Joy: Lasting Happiness
in a Changing World*
>>by Dalai Lama, Desmond Tutu,
>>and Douglas Carlton Abrams

*Leadership & Self-Deception:
Getting Out of the Box*
>by The Arbinger Institute

The Anatomy of Peace: Resolving the Heart of Conflict
>by The Arbinger Institute

Big Magic: Creative Living Beyond Fear
>by Elizabeth Gilbert

Goddesses Never Age
>by Christiane Northrup

*Eating in the Light of the Moon: How Women Can
Transform Their Relationship with Food Through
Myths, Metaphors, and Storytelling*
>by Anita A. Johnston, PhD

Diana, Herself: An Allegory of Awakening
>by Martha Beck

Acknowledgments

By far, this is the hardest part of this book for me to write. When I was a young child, I asked the Divine not to make me do this life alone, and I've been surrounded by amazing people my entire life. I can't name everyone here. If you are currently or have been in my life, I've been touched by you, and I'm grateful. Thank you.

At the same time, this book wouldn't be complete for me without specifically thanking the following people.

I have to start with those who gave me my start, my amazing family. Not only did it begin well with grandparents, parents (Alice and Jim), sisters (Molly and Anne), aunts, uncles, and cousins, but it just keeps getting bigger and better. We've added folks in every way imaginable, including my in-laws (Norman and Peg), and each person brings something unique and wonderful. You are my roots and my foundation, and I love being with you in any and every combination. Your place in my heart is sacred.

To my friends—especially Lori, Vicky, Elizabeth, Anne, and Deborah—laughing, crying, learning, walking, and talking, talking, talking with you is a true joy for me! You add such richness and sweetness to my life and help me know myself better. I won't even think about what my life would be like without you! I love you.

While I've been in and out of many groups, I've never been part of one as loving, intentional, committed, and fierce as the Crocodile leadership tribe. The love, magic, and transformation that I've witnessed and experienced has been life-changing. I had no idea that "leadership" meant shining a light on everything about yourself that you've tried to hide away, being fiercely and lovingly called to be a bigger version of yourself than you can imagine, and *experiencing* yourself as more than you dreamed you could be. And thank Heavens for it! My tribemates, I've given you my heart, and you've given me myself. You helped me become the person who could write this book. I love you, each and every one, and I'm grateful for you. You are mine, and I am yours. Special gratitude to my meditation partner and my fellow Croco-lotte goddesses. To our leadership team—L.A., Art, Isabella, and Claude—thank you for showing us the way and holding us as we found ours. You are forever a Crocodile.

I've had the amazing good fortune to work for and with two women who are leaders in their fields. Tapas Fleming, you taught me about spirituality, energy, and presence in such a deep way, and facilitated experiences that set me on a new course. I am very grateful. Christine Kane, you showed me how to take my spiritual work into the "real world" and to live it more boldly. You saw me, believed in me, coached me, and gave me a platform. I'm inspired by the way you teach through example and by consistently working on your own expansion. Without you, this book would have been much more "unicorns and rainbows" and much less practical. Thank you!

To the Angel coaches—Robbin, CSpring, Robin, Elaine, Whitney, Jen, and Kelly—Mwah!!! What a true joy to have served, laughed, and grown with you. You women are the bomb!

Coaches make a difference. Excellent coaches make a tremendous difference. I've had only excellent coaches. Thank you, Karen McMullen, Margo Bebinger, and Tery Elliot for your love, wisdom, and encouragement.

Maggie McReynolds, without your editing skills and encouragement, this book would still be a bunch of notes on my computer, living in the realm of "someday." Thank you for helping me show up and for midwifing this creation.

This book would not have happened without my wonderful clients. Your strength, vulnerability, courage, and questions have inspired me to dig deeper within myself and have brought up insights that I didn't know I had. Each of you has been a treasure and a gift, and I'm honored to have the pleasure of working with you.

Some people whom I only know through their books, recordings, and programs have still had a profound impact on my life. Panache Desai, Kyle Cease, Donna Eden, Glennon Doyle, Brené Brown, Martha Beck, Shonda Rhimes, and so many, many more, your words and work have taught me, supported me, made me cry, and made me laugh. Even more importantly, your showing up inspires me to do the same. Thank you for being so visibly yourself and sharing your work with the world.

And to my family:

Bri, my original little buddy, I love watching the way

you take on life. Your adventurous spirit and passion for changing the world will take you far.

Maylen, you are a force of nature. Life with you is an adventure full of laughter and fun. Watching you step up and own your power is one of my great joys. I can't wait to see what you decide to create with your life.

Someone just meeting the two of you might only see how different you are. I see how much you're alike in your humor, wisdom, courage, and loving heart. You two are an awesome duo. I couldn't be prouder of you, or love and enjoy you more.

Margaret Alice, you're my angel. Who knew that you could teach me so very much in such a short time.

All three of you have broken me open, called me up, and inspired a depth of love in me that I couldn't have imagined possible. You are my greatest teachers. The Universe loves me so fucking much that it wanted me to have daughters who would bring out my best, and so it gave me you.

Trey, you are a man of integrity, strength, caring, and fun. I can't imagine having done this life, with all of its ups and downs, with anyone else. You've seen me, believed in me, encouraged and supported me, and done a thousand things to make my life better. Thank you. I love you, sweet-myheart, and look forward to what we create from here.

Above all, I'm filled with gratitude that I am loved and held, in all ways and at all times, by All That Is. I want to say more and have restarted this sentence so many times, trying to find words to express the inexpressible. The words "thank you" are woefully, laughably inadequate for how I feel. Thankfully, the Divine doesn't need words to know what I mean. ♥

About the Author

Sara Arey is president and founder of **Refuture Your Life,** a company dedicated to empowering passionate entrepreneurs and creatives by dissolving seemingly impossible mindset blocks and old, unproductive patterns that stop success.

The basis of Sara's life-changing work is her Refuturing Process™, created after more than 25 years of studying

energy as a certified Reiki Master and a certified TAT®
Trainer, and working with private clients from more than
40 countries. Her tenure as the Education Director for
TATLife® and as a mindset coach for Uplevel You gave her
the opportunity to develop the skills and expertise that she
shares with her clients.

Sara leads clients through processes to release what's
holding them back and teaches them tools to continue
moving forward in their lives. Even more than that, Sara
uses her intuition and experience to take clients deep into
their hearts and souls to connect with their own inner
guidance and wisdom. Her clear energy and loving presence are a catalyst for others to make big shifts in how
they see themselves. Through making these shifts, Sara's
clients come into their power, take inspired action, and
create a present and future that wasn't possible before.

Visit

www.theuniversefuckinglovesme.com/gift
for the recording that accompanies this book.

You'll also find T-shirts, mugs, and more that say
"The Universe Fucking Loves Me"
and "What if it's possible..."

Made in the USA
Columbia, SC
28 May 2024

35953905R00104